NOTHING
BUT

NET

Published by CelebrityPress™, Orlando, FL
A division of The Celebrity Branding Agency®

Celebrity Branding® is a registered trademark
Printed in the United States of America.

ISBN: 9780985364342
LCCN: 2012937317

This publication is designed to provide accurate and authoritative information with regard to the subject matter covered. It is sold with the understanding that the publisher is not engaged in rendering legal, accounting, or other professional advice. If legal advice or other expert assistance is required, the services of a competent professional should be sought. The opinions expressed by the authors in this book are not endorsed by CelebrityPress™ and are the sole responsibility of the author rendering the opinion.

Most CelebrityPress™ titles are available at special quantity discounts for bulk purchases for sales promotions, premiums, fundraising, and educational use. Special versions or book excerpts can also be created to fit specific needs.

For more information, please write:

CelebrityPress™
520 N. Orlando Ave, #2
Winter Park, FL 32789

or call 1.877.261.4930

Visit us online at www.CelebrityPressPublishing.com

NOTHING
BUT

NET

Contents

CHAPTER 1

The Newest, Fastest, Easiest Way to Make Additional Big Money In Your Business!

By James Malinchak

Have you ever sat in a seminar listening to a speaker and while you were listening you said to yourself, "I bet he/she is making a lot of money talking about what they know!"…or…"I could do that"…or…"I would be so much better than that speaker if I were speaking!"

That's exactly how I began my entire speaking career. I remember sitting in an audience listening to a speaker talking about the most basic topic and wondering how much he was getting paid. After he finished his presentation, I asked if I could take him to lunch, which he kindly agreed. Over lunch, I let him tell me about his topic, as it was obvious he was passionate about it. Finally after 30-minutes into our lunch, I got enough courage to ask, "Could I ask how much you were just paid for delivering that 45-minute presentation?" To my surprise he said, "$10,000!"

What!?! I couldn't believe it! I was so shocked at the kind of money he was being paid for simply talking about something he knew!

Immediately, I knew I was going to start adding public speaking as a part of my business, even though I had no clue where to start or how to begin! And I can tell you now that looking back, making the decision to add public speaking to my current business was the absolute best business decision I ever made. Now,

I am on a mission to encourage and train as many business owners as possible to, not change their current business model, but to simply add public speaking as an add-on to their current business.

When you understand the power of adding public speaking to your current business and just how much more big money you can add to your bank account weekly, monthly and yearly, you will soon realize that you have been losing out on possibly hundreds of thousands of dollars. Hopefully, you will join those of us who understand that adding public speaking to your current business (whatever business you are in) can help you to tremendously build your business fast!

Let me share with you 6 reasons public speaking should be immediately added as a part of your business model!

1. *Credibility:* Would you like instant credibility as a "perceived" authority in your market? Or if you're already established in your market, would you like to instantly rise to the top as being thought of as the go-to person for your niche, product and service? Public speaking can instantly do that for you. When prospects have the chance to sit in a room and listen to you talk about a topic, instantly they assume you must be a leading authority/guru because you're the one speaking on the topic. You receive a level of credibility you can't get any other way.

2. *Free Publicity:* Newspapers, magazines and trade journals love to write free articles about you as they see you as an expert. They also call-on you to give quotes about certain topics for articles they are writing for their readers. Also, you are invited to write guest articles for subscribers.

3. *Paid Checks:* I am a top fee-paid speaker for corporations, associations, colleges, universities and youth organizations. I know some people may not desire getting paid checks for talking about what they know, but I love it! I think it's the coolest thing when you can get paid for a presentation talking about ideas that you would talk about anyway on a daily, weekly, monthly basis. And here's an added benefit. Not only can you get paid a check, but

you can also get to travel to some great resort areas while getting treated in a VIP first-class way. Gotta love it!

4. *Platform Offering:* There are many events where, although you may not be paid a check to speak, you can speak and offer your products to the audience in the form of continuing education so audience members can continue to learn from you after your talk is finished. You could offer continuing learning in the form of books, CDs, DVDs, home study courses, live seminar trainings, teleseminars, group mastermind coaching, one-on-one coaching, consulting, etc. When you deliver a talk filled with information that benefits the audience, many of them will want more of you and your ideas. It's your responsibility to allow audience members to continue learning from you so they can be better. And, you can make an incredible amount of extra money while helping a lot of people. I can't think of anything better in business – getting to talk about something that you enjoy that is helping audience members, while making big money.

5. *Spin-Off Business:* The spin-off business from public speaking can be amazing. What is spin-off business? Spin-off business is when you receive additional business opportunities from audience members. Imagine, you are giving a talk to a group talking on a topic you enjoy and when you finish, several audience members walk-up to you thanking you for a great talk. Then they ask if you would be able to give that same talk for their group. They can pay you a speaking fee (check) or they may not pay you a check but will allow you to offer your continuing education so their audience members can invest in themselves after your presentation. In addition to getting spin-off business from audience members, you can also get spin-off business from the original person or group who booked you to speak. They can re-book you for their next event or even book you for additional multiple events.

6. *Build Your List and an Immediate Following...FAST!* I love this one! When you speak to a group, you can immediately attract a group of raving fans who want to follow you and want to be marketed to by you. Public speaking is one of the best ways to start lead generation and list building because of the immediate connection audience members have with you.

Because you were the person who delivered the talk, audience members form a bond with you and see you as a credible source. They want to receive your emails and direct mail pieces. I still have people on my list buying products and attending my speaker boot camps who heard me speak 10 years ago to an audience.

Adding public speaking as a part of your current business is, by far, the BEST business decision you can make. It is, without a doubt, pound-for-pound, hour-for-hour, the best business model and the newest, fastest, easiest way to make additional big money in your business! And here's the good news, it's simply a learned skill that you can easily learn.

I've taken numerous business owners who had no clue how to start, where to begin or what they should even talk about, and showed them step-by-step a simple recipe to follow that had them making big money by simply talking about what they know. You can do it – the time is now! All you need to learn is the simple recipe!

About James

James Malinchak is called "Big Money Speaker®" and is recognized as "America's #1 Big Money Speaker Trainer & Coach for Anyone Who Wants to Make Big Money As a Highly Paid Public Speaker!"

James was Featured on ABC's Hit TV Show, "Secret Millionaire," and has delivered over 2,000 presentations for business groups, corporations, colleges and youth organizations worldwide for audiences ranging from 20 to 6,000 and has done so without being famous, any advanced academic degrees and without any speaker designations from any speaker associations.

He's written 10 books…including co-authoring the best-seller, Chicken Soup for the College Soul, and he was named Marketer of the Year by Marketing Guru's Dan Kennedy & Bill Glazer.

James owns 4 businesses, has read and researched over 3,000 books on personal and professional development. He also works with numerous celebrities, professional sports coaches and athletes and has even been interviewed on the Celebrity Red Carpet by Hollywood Interviewer Robin Leach.

If you've ever dreamed of making the kind of big money that only being a public speaker can bring you, then visit:

If you've ever dreamed of making the kind of big money that only being a public speaker can bring you, then visit:
www.BigMoneySpeaker.com
www.CollegeSpeakingSuccess.com
www.MillionaireSpeakerSecrets.com

CHAPTER 2

Show Up, Be Bold, Play Big

By Kim Hodous

I've been showing up, being bold and playing big since I was a kid. My mother loves to tell the story that when I was four I wouldn't let my friends eat grapes because I had overheard adults discussing how the migrant workers were being mistreated! I've always believed in the power of one person and our ability to make a difference. *Show up, be bold and play big*—it's these three simple strategies that have served as the basis for my abundant life and successful business.

I'd been a stay-at-home mom for seven years when I decided to turn my kitchen table hobby of making jewelry into a business. From the very beginning, I made the decision to show up, be bold and play big, and the results have been near miraculous. It's not that there haven't been bumps along the way, but when you have a simple strategy of how to succeed, the bumps don't bounce you quite as far or as high.

Showing up is about what to "do" in business and life. It's about actions we can take on a daily basis to wake up and be more present to all the opportunity and goodness around us. Being bold is about how to "be" in business. It's about character and strength and standing out from the crowd. Playing big is about how to "think" in business. To go somewhere you've never gone or to accomplish something that's bigger than you are, you've got to think a certain way and control and direct your thoughts. Combine those three strategies: showing up, being bold and playing big—and you've got a knock out formula for playing the game of business and living your life, at the highest level possible.

SHOW UP

To show up is to become fully engaged in your own life and business. Showing up is about waking up. It's about seeing all the possibility around you, and then doing something about it. Showing up is the "doing" part of the formula for success. But first you have to show up.

I was happily making bracelets at my kitchen table with my teenage daughters, when one day a friend asked to buy one to give as a gift. I could have simply obliged, pocketed the fifteen dollars and continued with my hobby. But I was paying attention, so I decided to test the waters with a homemade website.

Step No. 1 when you show up is to pay attention. Because I was paying attention two things happened. First, the administrative assistant to the CEO of a major corporation bought one from the website, and that CEO saw it on the wrist of her admin, and she loved it. She decided to focus a whole advertising campaign around that bracelet. I sold 2,000 bracelets of that one style to that company over the next two months. That was more bracelets than I sold the whole rest of that year.

Not only do you have to pay attention, but you need to pay attention to the things that matter. In business that means opportunities, your clients, your cash flow and your sales. In life, it's your family, your health and your spirit.

When you're paying attention, and you get an idea, the next step is to act on it. Walt Disney, the great American entrepreneur and entertainment icon said, "The way to get started is to stop talking and start doing." So once you've shown up in your business and you're paying attention—start doing!

The second major thing that happened early in my transition from hobby to business was another call from someone who had purchased one of my bracelets from that homemade website. This woman worked at the Jewish Community Center of Rochester, New York, and she wanted to know if they could sell the bracelets as a fundraiser. Without wasting a breath, I replied, "Well certainly. I'll get a fundraising packet right out to you." I had no idea what a fundraising packet was, but as soon as I hung up the phone I Googled, "jewelry fundraising." Fundraising was nowhere on my radar. But I was awake and paying attention, and I had a mind-set of movement. Within 48 hours I had a fundraising packet put together, and it was on its way to Rochester, New York!

Step 2 is to take *consistent* action. I was only selling about five bracelets a month online. But I was doing it every month consistently. It was those few early sales that launched everything. Start doing. Now. Cultivate a mind-set of movement.

Another part of showing up is to observe and listen. I listened when a friend asked to buy a bracelet. I listened when a client asked to sell my jewelry as a fundraiser. Today, 90 percent of my jewelry is sold through school, church and sports organization fundraisers. Once we're headed down a path, the direction will be revealed to us, if we'll just observe and listen. What if I hadn't been paying attention? What if I hadn't taken action and created a fundraising packet? Where are you missing opportunity in your business? Where are you missing joy in your life?

To pay attention to what matters, to take consistent action, and to observe and listen are just three of the things you can do to show up in your business and life.

BE BOLD

Being bold is your "state of being" in business. *Webster's Dictionary* defines bold as "standing out prominently; so as to be easily noticed." Being bold isn't about being loud or outrageous, or obnoxious or aggressive. It's about standing out in the crowd of competitors in your industry.

The first way to be bold is to be different. Find a way to set yourself apart from everyone else. When I started selling jewelry in fundraising, I only had one major difference from my competitors. My jewelry was custom-designed by me. All the other fundraising jewelry was being bought in China off a factory showroom floor. It wasn't specifically designed for and exclusively sold in the fundraising industry. It gave me the advantage because I could tailor my designs to what I knew would sell to that target market.

When you're being different, you must also be fearless. It's scary to do things differently than everyone else. It's scary to be the first one to test a new idea. But that's also where the payoffs are. You want to be risky but not reckless. Test the idea in small ways so you can get solid results to see if the idea will work. My first collection of fundraising jewelry had seven pieces. My competitors had jewelry collections of hundreds of styles. I started with seven. Seven! Those seven pieces lead to a collection the next year of 18 items.

Testing my idea in a small way had a big payoff. At the end of those two years, I increased my sales by 700 percent! To this day, I still have fewer than 50 designs in my collection annually, and the competitors that are still left in the industry, well they still have hundreds. I'm doing it differently than everyone else.

Another way to be bold is to be open. So many companies today, especially large ones, have established protocols, and their way is the only way. I believe one of our greatest opportunities is to be open to new ideas, developments and opportunities.

A few years into fundraising, I received a handwritten letter asking to see samples of my jewelry. The shaky writing made it look as though it had been written by my 70-year-old grandfather. Most people would have tossed that letter, but I followed up on it. That follow-up led to a mentorship with a man who helped me gain access to a trade show I'd been trying to attend for more than three years. As a result of attending that trade show, I booked $285,000 worth of sales. When we're open, we don't prejudge. I found out years later from my mentor that he had sent out more than 20 of those letters, and I was the only one who responded. There were at least 19 people who lost the opportunity to grow their businesses because they judged an old-fashioned handwritten letter. Be open.

Being bold is about standing out. It's about doing things in a different way and with a different mind-set than others. Be bold. Be different. Be fearless. Be open.

PLAY BIG

Playing big is about the "way you think." It's about mastering your mind and remembering that you're here for greatness. Playing big is about maximizing every bit of success, prosperity, joy and fun in your business—and your life. From the day I decided to turn my hobby into a business, when someone would ask what I did, I would respond with, "I'm president and CEO of a million-dollar company." Their eyes would widen, and they'd look enormously impressed. I would offer no explanation. I was president and CEO of a million-dollar company; it just hadn't fully arrived yet. That was my standard answer when my sales were only $4,000 annually! You can't expect to start out where you want to end up, but you must to know where you want to end up! To play big, you must dream big!

Dreaming big is one of the first steps to playing big. Your business will never rise higher than the vision you have for it. And for that matter, your life will never exceed your expectations of it. So you can't end up with a million-dollar business if your dream is to just be able to pay the bills. Your dream may be to simply supplement your income from a full-time job. Maybe it's to impact thousands of lives or change the nature of commerce in the world. Whatever it is, don't limit yourself. You can only play big if you dream big.

The next step for playing big is accepting 100 percent responsibility for where you are right now in your life and in your business. If you're going to play big, there can be no complaining, blaming, justifying, de-fending or excuse-making. The people who have made it to the top have done it by taking whatever life has handed them and worked with it. There are people with limited resources, capital and knowledge that are playing full out, and they're doing it by taking responsibility for their choices and where they are. If you want to play big, you must take re-sponsibility for your life and your business.

Gratitude is also essential for playing big. When we can be grateful for everything in our lives, we can open ourselves up to receive even more. Resistance is one of the main blocks to expansion. When we accept what comes our way, and then express gratitude for it, the sky truly is the limit. Think about the experiences in your life where you have grown the most. Weren't they the ones that were the most painful? When I ask that question, whether it's a crowd of 20 or 2,000, the response is always the same. All the hands go up. It's through the challenges that we grow. So why not appreciate them? They're there for our benefit. It's noble to be grateful for the good things that come our way, but if we want to play at an even higher level, we must also be grateful for the challenges in business. Gratitude enhances everything in life, especially our ability to play big.

To play big, you must dream big, take full responsibility for where you are, and express gratitude for all things in your business and in your life.

Life is an adventure. It's meant to be lived to the fullest. Business is just a part of life. Your life and your business will reflect the actions you take, the attitudes you hold and the thoughts you think on a daily basis. To show up, be bold and play big are three simple strategies you can use to experience more success in every area of your life. Show up. Be bold. Play big. The world is waiting for you!

About Kim

As a former high school history teacher, Kim Hodous had zero business experience. However, she went on to build a seven-figure business from her kitchen table. Her jewelry pieces have appeared in over 10 million catalogs, and her client list boasts names such as American Greetings, *Reader's Digest,* and Nivea Skincare. Her work was recognized in 2007 when she was inducted into the Arkansas Small Business Hall of Fame.

What she discovered through the rise of her business—from being a stay-at-home mom to being a CEO—is that how we show up creates a chain reaction that sets into motion predictable outcomes. When she looks back at every successful sale, every miraculous thing that happened in her business, she knows she set the stage for that by how she showed up. She's now sharing that knowledge to help you learn how to show up, be bold and play big so you can experience a level of success greater than you ever have before.

As a popular speaker, Kim's presentations have taken her from intimate groups of 20 to conferences of 2,000. She shares her message of showing up, being bold and playing big, along with her original and unique material on work and life balance. Aside from being an author, Kim is also a sought after one-on-one coach and business mentor.

Kim's fun and no-nonsense style will help you show up, be bolder and play bigger than you ever have before. Please go to www.kimhodous.com to learn more about Kim's books, products, coaching and speaking. You can contact her at me@kimhodous.com or (888) 784-7489.

CHAPTER 3

Cutting Through Complicated Situations to Create Simple Solutions

By Paul Prestwich, Ph.D.

Consider the following quotes: The Irish playwright George Bernard Shaw said, "For every complex problem, there is a simple solution that is wrong." However, Ronald Reagan, 40th U.S. president, argued the following: "They say the world has become too complex for simple answers. They are wrong."

What to make of these competing quotes? Well, Shaw supported Stalin but opposed the smallpox vaccination, while Reagan was instrumental in ending the Cold War with the Soviet Union. I'll go with Reagan overall. While most complex problems do indeed have many simple incorrect attempts at "solutions," *a great leader cuts through complicated situations to create simple, effective solutions.*

For small-business owners and leaders of larger organizations alike, complicated situations abound. Strategic initiatives and the problems associated with their implementation can be multifarious. In these situations, you may be tempted to put forward solutions that are equally complex. Great leaders, however, understand that the ability to analyze complicated information—and then generate laser-like solutions—is a foundation for personal and organizational success.

A SIMPLE SOLUTION TO AN ENROLLMENT CHALLENGE

Colleges and universities are complicated organizations with multiple funding sources, unclear and competing goals, and complex power structures. Woodrow Wilson, 28th President of the United States, had been president of Princeton University earlier in his career. Noting the difficulty of enacting change in such a setting, Wilson argued, "It is easier to change the location of a cemetery than to change the school curriculum."

Because they have significant inertia—which makes simple breakthroughs difficult—higher education can provide good examples of leaders who create simple solutions in spite of organizational complexities.

In the early 2000s, the president of a midsize community college in the northeast United States recognized a need to increase enrollment following years of slow growth. But enrollment management is a complex process, in part because a college doesn't have immediate feedback as to what works and what doesn't. Only when the new class of freshmen shows up in the fall (that's right, just once a year) does the institution understand how well the diversity of activities—in which they engaged during the previous 12 months—worked.

One simple solution, though, led to an immediate surge in enrollment: Instead of beginning the fall term a week or two before Labor Day, like most other institutions of higher education, the college decided to start the fall term *after* Labor Day. Enrollment in the subsequent fall term increased dramatically.

Why did this solution work?

University students, after being admitted, are required to decide long before mid-August where they plan to attend. Not so for many community college students. *Community college students* typically make a final decision regarding where, or if, they plan to attend college much later than university students, and they're often in need of more financial support than university students. Thus, community colleges that start even just a couple weeks later than mid-August give interested students longer to make a decision and, perhaps more important, give them longer to earn money in the summer.

In addition, within the first few weeks of each fall semester, thousands of new university freshmen nationwide realize that they don't like their chosen university. Many decide to enroll instead in community colleges, a phenomenon called a "reverse transfer." If the community college's fall term starts a week or two following the start of the university's fall term, "reverse transfers"—even within the same *fall term*—are much easier.

Why Is Simplicity a Desirable Goal?

There are at least four positive aspects to a successful, simple solution:

- *Simple ideas drive great organizations.* Simple ideas and solutions are easier to communicate to your employees, customers, clients and stakeholders. Colin Powell has stated, "Great leaders are almost always great simplifiers, who can cut through argument, debate and doubt to offer a solution everybody can understand."[1]

- *Simple solutions are easier and more efficient to implement.* The more complex an attempted solution is, the more likely that it will fail or—perhaps even worse in the long run—be mediocre. In engineering terms, the more moving parts a machine has, the more energy is lost due to friction between the parts. The same is true with organizations.

- *Simple solutions are easy to replicate.* Simple solutions enable organizations to be more *consistently* successful.

- *Simple solutions are faster to implement.* As will be discussed further later in this chapter, speed is the currency of success.

11 KEYS FOR CREATING SIMPLE, SUCCESSFUL SOLUTIONS

Having discussed why simple solutions are important, here are the 11 keys for creating simple and successful solutions. The first four are *what simple solutions aren't*. These are critical to understand prior to building a solutions-oriented organization. The next three keys build the *foundation* for creating great solutions. Once these necessary considerations are in place, four intertwined factors—called *breakthrough accelerators*—lead to long-term success and competitiveness.

What Simple Solutions Aren't

Before discussing the strategies involved in cutting through complicated situations to create simple solutions, let's define what simple solutions *aren't*:

1. *A simple solution isn't necessarily the easiest alternative.* Creating simple solutions is rarely just a question of ease, although simply effective solutions might require relatively little effort. But ease should not be your overriding factor. Many highly damaging mistakes are made because the desired action was expedient and undemanding.

2. *A simple solution isn't necessarily the least expensive.* Simple solutions might be inexpensive. This was the case in the college example, which had virtually no cost. But as any good leader knows, the least expensive attempt at a solution in the short run, if approached incorrectly, might be the most expensive over the long run.

3. *A simple solution isn't necessarily the one that uses the most technology.* Too often I hear leaders, whether at large organizations or at small businesses, discuss the increased use of technology (and the resulting increases in costs) as though the technology itself creates a solution *when leaders can't even describe what value it actually adds.* Based on his landmark research on companies that made transformations to greatness, Jim Collins argued that for those companies, appropriate application of technology was used to *speed improvement that already existed.* It was never the *principal driver* of greatness.[2]

4. *A simple solution isn't the right answer to the wrong problem.* Some simple "solutions" aren't solutions that truly help an organization. They're answers to a perceived problem that has been incorrectly or insufficiently identified. I'm reminded of the old saying: "Some kind of 'help' is the kind of help we all can do without."

The Foundation: I/Q/RP

Leaders need to understand that before successful planning can occur or any solution successfully implemented, three key factors must be firmly in place: *information, quality*, and the *right people*.

I'll call these I/Q/RP. The late George Keller—a successful higher education leader, consultant and author—discussed these factors in his influential book on planning within the context of higher education, *Academic Strategy,* which has applicability beyond higher education.[3] The best information, an emphasis on quality, and having the right people in the right positions are necessary conditions for creating great, streamlined solutions to complicated issues. If these three factors aren't strong in your organization, you may as well forget about enacting great solutions. You'll waste time and money chasing possible solutions if your organizational foundation isn't strong.

5. ***Seek out the best information.*** Whether you lead a large, complicated organization, or you're an entrepreneur with a staff of two part-timers, you need to truly understand the organization you lead. *Actively seeking out the best information—and then processing it with keen insight—can, by itself, lead to simple breakthroughs.*

A great leader should always be able to answer these questions: What's happening from a quantitative standpoint? What's happening from a qualitative standpoint?

Great leaders know how to ask the right questions. Great leaders know how to exhibit the indispensable communication technique of *listening.*

The challenges here are significant. Many entrepreneurs, for example, struggle because they don't understand simple ideas like the value of their time, and thus they spend too much of it on tasks that could be outsourced or assigned elsewhere, instead of on revenue-generating activities. Leaders of larger organizations often pay too little attention to critical information or spend too little time interacting with employees to learn what *really* works and what the true issues are. There are countless mediocre leaders who receive seemingly endless analyses, cutting data every way possible. However, *if those analyses are answering the wrong questions, they're virtually useless.*

6. ***Demand quality.*** You should demand that every aspect of the organization is of the highest quality. Quality breeds quality.

I'm not talking about any particular management theory, such as Total Quality Management. *I'm talking about promoting the kind of quality throughout the organization that would meet your grandmother's approval.*

7. *Hire the right people and get rid of those who aren't cutting it.* Virtually all management and leadership experts recognize the importance of having the *right people* in the *right positions* in your organization. Regardless of the size of your organization, place your best employees in positions that strengthen your group. It's much more important to focus on strengths and opportunities than on weaknesses. Your staffing should reflect that.

Perhaps as important, get rid of people who aren't the right fit for your organization. Addition by subtraction might violate the principles of mathematics, but the practice is almost always an integral aspect of organizational health and success.

You shouldn't be spared from a careful examination of your human resources. Although it's more of an issue for small-business entrepreneurs than it is for CEOs of larger organizations, sometimes you need to *fire yourself.* Of course, you won't fire yourself from your position completely, but if you're trying to do things that others can do better—or less expensively—you need to have an authentic conversation with yourself. Look in the mirror and tell yourself that you're "moving in a different direction."

Once a leader and/or entrepreneur implements the principles of I/Q/RP, planning and solution-building will be more effective. I/Q/RP is the foundation. Now let's build a solutions-oriented operation...

The Breakthrough Accelerators

8. *Think in reverse.* The Greek philosopher Epictetus said, "First say to yourself what you would be; and then do what you have to do." Leaders should ask first and foremost, *What would their organization be?* When that question is answered and communicated, solutions are more likely because any potential solution will be an answer to the *right* question. Remember: Great leaders are great simplifiers. One way that's accomplished is to ensure that vision drives strategy and solution-building, not vice versa.

Too many organizations' goals are essentially a collection of numerical targets that exists in a vacuum that should have been filled with an overarching vision. But leaders who create an organizational "fabric" that supports the creation of simple, successful solutions understand that the creation of a grand vision—which is also communicated effectively—drives strategy and activity.

9. *Create organizational alignment.* Alignment between vision and strategy creates organizational integrity. Just as personal integrity tends to cause personal success, organizational integrity creates an environment where solutions are more likely to be offered, agreed upon and thrive. Picture an individual with integrity—they know who they are and where they're going. Organizations with appropriate alignment are similar. Alignment doesn't answer all questions, but simple solutions thrive in that environment. On the other hand, if you want to run the risk of promoting one of George Bernard Shaw's "wrong solutions," simply pay little attention to organizational alignment and integrity.

10. *Focus on speed.* When an organization thinks in reverse and has alignment and integrity, it must act quickly. Speed kills. Well, it kills your competition. This isn't an issue for only large organizations. Sometimes even small businesses implement strategies and react to market trends far too slowly. (This is one of the reasons that most small businesses fail within the first few years.)

Jack Welch, the famed CEO and chairman of General Electric for 20 years, understood the power of speed: "Speed is everything. It is the indispensable ingredient of competitiveness."[4]

One might argue that acting impulsively can create problems for an organization. It's certainly possible that speed can create problems if organizations act without understanding their strengths and advantages in their industry. That's acting like a squirrel, jerking from one short-term goal to the next. The speed I'm talking about is that of gazelle: undeniably fast and agile, with great endurance over a long distance.

Remember, speed can *sometimes* be a problem (if it's unfocused), but slowness almost always is.

11. *Simplify the organization.* Organizational simplicity—whether in small business or larger organizations—is closely intertwined with speed. When leaders simplify their organizations and build confidence in employees' abilities to make recommendations and implement improvements, they create businesses that not only *act* fast, but *think* fast.

Simple breakthroughs are unlikely to happen in cumbersome, overly complex, and bureaucratic organizations. Again, it might be tempting to think of this as an issue for only larger organizations, but even some small businesses are much too complex in relation to their scope.

LESSONS LEARNED

In conclusion, it pays to understand *what simple solutions simply aren't*. Build a culture that promotes I/Q/RP. Remember that once the *foundation* is in place, the quartet of *breakthrough accelerators*—i.e., thinking in reverse, creating alignment, acting with speed, and simplifying the organization—will provide a culture where simple solutions can be created to address complex problems and situations.

Notes

1. Oren Harari, *The Leadership Secrets of Colin Powell*
   (New York: McGraw-Hill, 2002).
2. Jim Collins, *How Great Companies Tame Technology,*
   available at www.jimcollins.com.
3. George Keller, *Academic Strategy: The Management Revolution in American Higher Education*
   (Boston & London: The Johns Hopkins University Press, 1983).
4. Janet C. Lowe, *Jack Welch Speaks: Wisdom from the World's Greatest Business Leader*
   (New York: John Wiley & Sons, 1998).

About Paul

Dr. Paul Prestwich is a leadership consultant and president of Northwest College in Powell, Wyoming. He has held positions of professor, dean and vice president at several institutions of higher education. He has also been a planning specialist for School of Medicine at the University of Pennsylvania, where he earned his Ph.D.

In addition to serving as the CEO of a $30 million, multi-site organization, he's the author of the books *Leadership Lessons You Won't Learn in the Classroom* and *The College Success Bible.* He provides speaking, consulting, and coaching services to businesses, colleges and universities, nonprofit organizations and youth organizations.

To learn more about the services Paul offers, visit *www.paulprestwich*, email *info@paulprestwich.com*, or call (800) 697-0876.

CHAPTER 4

The Ultimate Creative Problem Solving Process: Aligning Your Right and Left Brain

Dr. Paula Joyce

"For a long time, I've been wanting to _____."
You probably had difficulty finishing that sentence. Most of us don't like admitting to the goals we haven't achieved. Well, the truth is, you haven't failed. You just haven't had the right information. You've been working with only half your brain, the logical half. When you engage the other side of your brain, you'll tap into a huge reservoir of information—the part of you that knows the answers but can't communicate them.

The key to your success is to align the right and left sides of your brain. There's a war going on inside of you. It's as if two horses are pulling a cart in opposite directions. Until both horses are working together, you'll have constant obstructions and disappointments. When your right and left brain become partners, instead of adversaries, your power will ignite and you'll meet your goal with more speed and ease than you ever imagined. If you've been wondering what's wrong with you because you haven't accomplished your goal, the answer is: nothing. Your brain is just not fully aligned. The Ultimate Creative Problem Solving Process will get the power of both sides of your brain going in the same direction for your success.

My unique process is effective for health, wealth and relationships in your personal and business life. I've been using it successfully for 11 years with individuals, couples, leadership teams, boards, corporations, professional groups and groups of people at public seminars ranging in size from a handful to hundreds. Regardless of the purpose or size of the group, people consistently gain new insights, make breakthroughs, release hidden blockages and fears, reduce stress, solve their most challenging problems and increase their joy, productivity and success.

THE ULTIMATE CREATIVE PROBLEM SOLVING MODEL

The left brain is the logical, sequential and conscious side of our mind. The right side is creative, intuitive and unconscious. The left brain communicates with words and the right with images. Neither side understands the other. Although we generally think with our left brain, 10 million times more information resides in the right brain. You're actually handicapping yourself if you don't access this information and harness it for your benefit.

With my process, you go directly into the right brain, get the information you need and translate it so the left brain can understand it. You use your whole brain, allowing each side to do what it does best and to communicate with the other.

Usually the logical/conscious mind has total control. It has so many messages from our past that it's hard to hear the "still small voice" that's desperately trying to communicate. This process quiets the overactive left brain long enough to receive information from the right. By using crayons, you bring up the information from the unconscious that you need. You write to bring this information to conscious awareness. Then you discuss the images and the words to fully understand and integrate the messages from both sides of the brain.

While doing the crayoning and writing, you must not let the part of you that's skeptical, judging and intrusive get control and derail you. When her left brain is trying to pull her off-track, one of my clients says to it: "Thank you for sharing. Now, please take a seat on the couch and just listen." Determine what works for you and silence the "judge" in your mind.

The crayoning is only to access unconscious knowledge. It's not about creating a great work of art. It won't be framed or hung in a museum. It can be scribbles, shapes, lines, colors, stick figures, recognizable or unrecognizable images. It's the process, not the product, that counts.

Preceding the writing with crayoning takes you deeper inside yourself. The written word only deals in the realm of the conscious, and thus, is not as powerful when used without the crayoning.

Receiving the unconscious information and bringing it into your conscious awareness is a tremendous gift. When you see, read and ultimately "get" the message, you become totally aligned with it. You get it on all levels: spiritual, emotional, physical and mental. There's no part of you that can still hide from the Truth. Now the part of you that wants the very best for you is in charge and directing you to actualize your highest good. A path opens whereby your thoughts, words and actions are all aligned, allowing you to easily and naturally make the best decisions for you—the ones that will result in achieving the goals that will bring you true happiness and fulfillment.

THE ULTIMATE CREATIVE PROBLEM SOLVING PROCESS

1. Gather your materials: a box of crayons, plain white paper, and a pen or pencil.

2. Follow these steps:

   a) Identify the specific problem or goal that you want to work with in this session.

   b) Ask yourself: What is blocking me from solving my problem/achieving my goal?

      1. Crayon

      2. Write

      3. Discuss

   c) Ask yourself: What do I need to do now to solve my problem/achieve my goal?

      1. Crayon

      2. Write

      3. Discuss

   d) Summarize the information to align both sides of your brain.

1. *Crayon:* You have total freedom to create whatever you want. I suggest you allow yourself to begin with no idea of what you're going to do. Just pick whatever color you are drawn to and begin. Let your hand and/or heart guide you, not your mind. Allow the process to evolve without judging what it looks like. If you have trouble beginning, close your eyes, pick a crayon, put a mark on the paper, and allow the process to flow from there. When you create without the end in mind, you're going straight into your unconscious where the harvest is the richest. Let go to the process and reap the rewards.

2. *Write:* Write whatever comes into your mind. It could be anything from a list of words or thoughts to a poem or a story. Just allow yourself to write freely without stopping and without judging what you're writing. It doesn't have to make sense. You might even begin with: "This is stupid" or "I don't know what to write." Just begin with whatever comes into your mind. It will lead you to what you need to know.

Crayoning and Writing: When answering the two questions, some people go back and forth between crayoning and writing. That's fine as long as you always: 1) begin with crayoning because you want to "hear" the right brain first, and 2) do both crayoning and writing to integrate and align both sides of the brain.

During the crayoning and the writing, it's very important to silence the judge inside you and to get on paper whatever comes into your mind. Do this even if it looks ugly, stupid, childish or if it sounds unrelated or silly or whatever else the critic inside of you is saying. That's the voice that's trying to keep you away from what you really need to know. You can count on the critical voice being the one you should ignore. This is counter to our usual tendency to let the fear direct our lives. Here you have an opportunity to silence that voice and give the leadership role to the voice that directs you to healing, joy and success.

My clients often talk about being compelled to draw or write something even when they have tried to ignore the impulse. Usually they had judged it as something that was bad or silly. Invariably it carries a positive message. It brings a message that heals and creates good feelings, hope and release from past sadness, fears or hurts. Trust what's coming to you, even if it doesn't make sense or seems bad. It's important information that your Limitless Higher Self wants you to know.

Some of the information will begin to come together during the discussion part of this process. It is then that you will integrate the information from the crayoning and the writing. For now, just accept it as it is and be grateful for the wisdom that's coming to you. Crayon or write it down with complete abandon—or as much as you can gather in the moment.

3. **Discuss:** After completing the crayoning and writing for each question, talk to someone you trust about what you did. Share only what feels safe. If something comes up that's too sensitive to share, try to find a portion of your writing and/or crayoning or thoughts that you can offer for discussion. Look for ways that the crayoning and writing work together to create meaning. The crayoning may be symbolic. There might be a shape, an image, a symbol, a color or an overall feeling—something in the crayoning that creates meaning by itself or when connected to the writing. Sometimes the crayoning is unintelligible and doesn't appear to have any independent meaning. If so, its sole purpose, at least for the moment, is to allow information to emerge from the unconscious that will be conveyed to you through the writing.

The discussion partner's role is to be curious, ask questions and treat everything that you do and say with the utmost respect. If they have some thoughts that might be helpful to you, they may ask your permission to share them. You have the right to say yes or no. If they share something, determine if it feels like Truth to you. They may have something valuable to add or they may be pulling you off track. That's for you to decide. If you're uncertain, write it down and review it in the future. Sometimes we reject new information without processing it fully or it may be something that you are not yet ready to hear. In a month or so it may resonate with you or it may truly not be relevant to you ever.

Hopefully you can find someone in your life with whom you can share with total trust and who's trustworthy in return. If not, you might want to find a professional coach or counselor to talk with about your crayoning and writing.

4. *Summarize:* Write a short summary integrating the information from your crayoning and drawing. Add insights gained by seeing the shifts from your first crayoning and writing to your second. If there are actions that you want to take as a result of what you learned, write those down, too.

A FEW SUCCESS STORIES

Even if you know what's blocking your success, you need to use the process to integrate the information within both sides of your brain. Once you have total alignment, the chaos of indecision and uncertainty releases and new energy and freedom emerge. Dramatic results can come slowly over time or quickly in a session or two. It all depends on the organization or the company. Below are a few examples of real clients' successes.

- One company's leadership team solved their unique problem regarding communication. Since many of their employees are off-site, typical techniques weren't working. In two hours we designed a system that was so successful that the CEO uses The Ultimate Creative Problem Solving Process at every leadership team meeting.

- Amanda believed that her boss did not like her. Her right brain showed her she was a perfectionist, which prevented her from meeting deadlines. She realized she was in control of her success and went from despair to being a company star.

- A nonprofit was floundering. I led their board retreat, which resulted in a redesigning of their mission statement, internal structure and strategic plan. This led to positive energy, increased membership, successful collaborations and new leadership coming forward.

- John had been trying for two years to figure out how to get a $60,000 software package that he couldn't afford. In just one session, he realized he could offer to prove the effectiveness of the software in exchange for a complimentary copy. The next day, he successfully made the deal.

- Alicia had been suffering from a sinus infection for numerous months despite strong antibiotics. Her counselor felt it would clear if she could cry over the incest she had experienced. In our session, her unconscious guided her to draw a tear, which led to her letting herself cry and her return to good health.

- When James came to me, he owed the IRS thousands of dollars, was in a failing business with an abusive partner, and was an alcoholic who said he'd never go to AA. He now is sober and a committed participant in AA, has a well-paying job, is enjoying a healthy love relationship, is out of debt and is pursuing ways to invest his savings.

The Ultimate Creative Problem Solving Process feels like a gift from my right brain, and I'm grateful for it. People come to me with the weight of the world on their shoulders and leave smiling. I hope using this process does the same for you.

About Paula

Dr. Paula Joyce, The Life Doctor, has helped thousands of people improve their health, wealth and relationships through her writing, coaching and speaking. Paula's clients attain success, achieve breakthrough thinking and enhance productivity by working with her Ultimate Creative Problem Solving Process to align and integrate the information in the right and left sides of their brain. This allows them to dissolve hidden fears and barriers, solve their most challenging problems and reach their goals.

As someone who has faced many challenges in life, Paula walks her talk. Despite being told that she would never be able to dance, paint or write creatively, she has become an accomplished Argentine Tango dancer, an artist whose work is shown in museums around the world, and an author whose creative writing and poetry have been published. Despite being raised to believe that a woman should never get too much education, work while raising children, or be successful in a career, Paula did postdoctoral work at Yale University in the Cognitive Psychology Department and was Director of Leadership Development for the Carrollton-Farmers Branch Independent School District where she coached and trained top level executives. She has overcome emotional and psychological abuse and taught herself to see the positive in every experience and feel the gratitude for all of it.

An internationally published and translated author, her most recent book, *33 Tips for Self-Empowerment*, is available as an e-book and will soon be in print. Her next book, *Tango: The Dance of Life*, is in preparation. Go to her website and sign up for her newsletter to be among the first to receive a publication notice.

Paula uses her Ultimate Creative Problem Solving Process with such diverse organizations as American Express Financial Services, Baylor University Medical Center, The Jung Society, Voluntary Hospital Association, The Women's Museum and Right Management Consultants.

Some of the topics that Paula presents to national and international audiences are leadership development, team building, wellness, de-stressing, life transitions, conflict resolution, change management, overcoming abuse/self empowerment, strategic planning, positive thinking, life after divorce, nourishment of the spirit, from fear to freedom and staying mentally sharp.

Paula has been in *The Dallas Morning News* and on national radio and television. You can listen to podcasts of her radio show, "Uplift Your Life With Dr. Paula," on her website or iTunes.

If you want to actualize your true potential with more ease, visit Paula at:
www.PaulaJoyce.com
www.PaulaJoyceDesigns.com

CHAPTER 5

The *Passion to Profits* Entrepreneur: "Black Belt" Strategies for Making Money While Making a Difference

By Stephen Whittier

"Success begins with belief in your vision and the inevitability of its attainment; is fed by your desire to acquire and apply the right knowledge and tools to achieve it; and is actualized through focused, consistent implementation of that knowledge."

With a nod to the *Beatles*, it's fair to say my journey into entrepreneurship has been quite the "long and winding road"—born out of a strange series of career transitions that ran the gamut from professional educator to martial arts instructor-turned studio owner before becoming a full-fledged businessman.

In the early days I was pretty sensitive about how all this would be perceived. When asked what I did for a living, I once enjoyed a degree of social respectability in saying, "I teach at the university." I received a much a different response, however, once I started explaining that I *used* to teach at the university but had jumped on the entrepreneurial path to follow my first passion, which was helping people to enhance their lives through the vehicle of martial arts and fitness.

For most people, the mental image of an ivory tower lecturer shedding tweed and khakis to run around barefoot teaching others how to punch, kick and grapple would seem a bit insane. That was perception, then there were the stark realities of business. Search *Wikipedia* for the definition of "rude awakening," and you're apt to read the cautionary tale of a respected young academic and decorated martial arts instructor who ventures into business chock-full of pep, vinegar, and great ideas—only to find that the marketplace could give a hot damn about his opinions, credentials, or GPA.

In hindsight, I now realize that my unlikely background was actually a strength, and my seemingly polar-opposite career tracks were actually congruent in many ways: Whether teaching academics or martial arts, for instance, my role has encompassed that of educator, researcher, motivator, critical thinker, and—at the core—success coach.

These experiences also allowed me learn how *not* to be just another small-business owner who started a brick and mortar operation doing what he was good at. Instead, I've learned how to successfully leverage and monetize my true passions while helping others through my service as an entrepreneur. Today, as an owner of both successful physical and online businesses, I've been able to once again leverage my skills sets in teaching, performance coaching, business ownership and marketing to assist other aspiring entrepreneurs in transforming their own interests into income.

Now let's dig into some of the core principles behind entrepreneurial success. Even though each of these could easily constitute a full-length book by itself, my aim is to break down some of the most crucial elements into a concise, easily digestible format.

BLACK BELT SUCCESS STRATEGY #1: YOU MUST GET YOUR MIND RIGHT FIRST!

Don't worry, this isn't going to be another self-help article. In fact, I'm often quite critical of the whole "motivational speaker" genre in general. Exceptions are great speaker coaches like James Malinchak, who's refreshing to me because he bucks industry norms by using his platform not only to inspire but also deliver *concrete, actionable business strategies* to his seminar attendees.

Motivation and inspiration are no doubt very important for entrepreneurs, especially during the dark times when you feel like you're clawing your way through the wilderness. As a businessman, though, I desire more than eloquently delivered rhetoric designed to whip an audience into a frenzy of enthusiasm (because that wave of energy inevitably breaks and begins to fade). For the practical minded, continued motivation is fueled by real, applicable *knowledge*.

There's a flip side to this, however; after muddling along through trial and error for some time after starting out in business, I ultimately had to admit that just as motivation without knowledge is an empty proposition, the opposite is also true:

> *Without a clearly defined vision of your goals,*
> *knowledge alone won't be enough to attain them.*

Let me give you an example. Consider the terms "entrepreneur" and "small-business owner." While these tend to be used interchangeably, and no doubt many entrepreneurs are also proprietors of small businesses, ask yourself if there's a difference between the two—and if so, which are you?

I've come to find that entrepreneurs are something of a different breed; they not only think differently in terms of how they *execute within* their business, but they think differently *about* their business. And to be sure, they *act* differently…they adopt and live by a unique set of habits.

My point here isn't to over-romanticize entrepreneurism. But while it isn't rocket science by any stretch, neither is it straightforward or simple. And there are indeed "secrets of the trade." Those who fail to learn them (choosing instead to live according to myths like "work hard doing what you love and the rest will take care of itself") are usually setting themselves up to fail.

The reason for this is a phenomenon I call "SASR" for short: *Same Actions = Same Results*

It's the natural tendency, even among highly impassioned and motivated entrepreneurs, to slip into familiar, comfortable patterns. And no matter how much you try to convince yourself that you're the exception, that your current level of inspiration will carry you through indefinitely, I guarantee you it's a delusion.

Acknowledging this, it becomes the entrepreneur's job each and every day to break the cycle of those "same actions," which means being clearly anchored at all times to a well-defined vision and plan for attaining it. If there's one immutable "secret" I can give to anyone looking to pursue the entrepreneurial life, it is this: Just as a business isn't a proper business without a business plan, *your vision of success is nothing unless you have defined it, written it down, regularly review it, and set a time limit on it!*

BLACK BELT SUCCESS STRATEGY #2: THE THREE "I'S" OF SUCCESS

In my martial arts organization, we employ a simple but very effective, three-step training progression for taking students from the initial, rote learning of techniques to the application of those techniques in real time. A great performance coach and friend of mine coined this approach the "I Method."

Now when it comes to performance coaching, whether we're talking about business or Brazilian jiu-jitsu, every profession has similar concerns: "What do we need to do to move from theory and knowledge to application and results?" So after 20-plus years in the martial arts, it made sense to me to create an analogous methodology for entrepreneurial success, one that distills it all down to the essential components:

Investment

For an entrepreneur, the notion of investment reaches far beyond small-business loans or venture capital. What I mean by the term has to do with investing in and acquiring what Napoleon Hill referred to as "specialized knowledge"—think *intellectual* capital. And as Hill was careful to note, this isn't the type of knowledge you're likely to get in any college course.

That's why the most successful entrepreneurs all have their own coaches, mentors and peers who are "out in the field" themselves. That's also why they take seminars, purchase home-study courses, and read books like this one while others play video games or chat on web forums about the latest batch of "American Idol" hopefuls (again, a different set of habits).

I'll cite my own entry into information marketing as testimony for the power of investing in yourself. Given my academic background I had quite a bit of experience with writing; after college I even managed to parlay that skill into writing ad copy for a time—at a *very* modest salary. While copywriting was much different than writing grad school papers, I quickly got the knack once I figured out what most clients wanted, which was for their ad copy to read like everyone else's.

Fast forward to my first online product release years later. As a direct result of investing in the right resources and guidance, my very first sales letter generated nearly $60,000 in sales—half of that *in the first four days*. If anything was a positive affirmation of doing things differently, that was it! Now, the knowledge I've gained has led others from a variety of industries to seek me out for joint venture opportunities and coaching on how to market their own products. There's no doubt that if I had simply stuck with the old copywriting formula, those "same actions" would have yielded the same results as before.

Here's a critical take away for you: Smart entrepreneurs avoid "business as usual" like the plague. Instead, they: a) eagerly invest in learning the tools (and finding the people) to get them to the next level, and b) value *results* above personal opinion and decades of trial and error.

Implementation

I must plead with you to read, and then re-read this next line until it sticks:

> *No matter how much you invest or how much specialized knowledge you gain, it is absolutely meaningless if you don't implement it.*

And make no mistake: The most effective implementation is always *fast* implementation. This is of the utmost importance to grasp because there's just no way around it. In fact, speed of implementation is the single ingredient that often separates wild success from total obscurity.

Another one of those singular habits exhibited by entrepreneurs, maybe the most important of all, is our tendency to act on good information with equal parts urgency (*"Start it NOW!"*) and focus (*"Get it done!"*).

Bottom Line: "Analysis paralysis" is your enemy! Don't try to nail down all the details first—as entrepreneurs we'll figure those out as we go, test the results, adapt and make adjustments as necessary. Although this fast action, "leap before you look" strategy may not be recommended for all fields of endeavor (cliff diving comes to mind…), to be a successful entrepreneur it's the "secret" habit you *must* master.

Influence

Finally, we come to the effect that rapid implementation of specialized knowledge produces: *influence*.

The critical thing to grasp about influence is that most people's understanding of it is completely backward…conventional wisdom (which should generally be avoided at all costs) would have you believe that influence is waiting on the horizon, magically to appear once all the necessary conditions have fallen into place. This is another dangerous delusion.

Here's the real secret of influence: *You have to claim it in order to possess it*. In other words, consider the habits, posture and means by which other successful entrepreneurs hold influence. Once you have defined those, you must adopt, embody, and above all, learn to effectively *market* those very same qualities. Starting now!

And swinging full circle back to the importance of vision, it should be clear that by "marketing" I'm not talking about some sort of snake-oil transaction. Your value in business comes from your expertise in delivering products or services that are of *great value to others*. The notion of "passion to profits" is about making money while making a difference—and no one is better suited than the entrepreneur to monetize one's passions. In business, marketing (and creating influence around) your vision, your mission, your story and your unique positioning is everything.

BLACK BELT SUCCESS STRATEGY #3:
EMBRACE THE GRIND!

This last tip is brief and to the point but cannot be overemphasized: Being an entrepreneur is a straight-up *grind*.

There's no avoiding this fact (at least not that I've seen), so it's best to accept it going in. But also know this…as much of a grind as it can be, it's your grind. When it comes to personal goals, entrepreneurship is about your quest for personal and financial autonomy.

It's crucial to remember this when the going gets tough, because it *will* get tough at times. The question is, especially in an era where we have record numbers of college graduates entering a shrinking job market (with most already in massive debt), do you want to endure those tough times on your own terms, or at the mercy of others?

I, for one, am looking to help those kindred spirits who are fighting for the driver's seat!

For more information on Stephen's marketing services and success coaching programs, and to receive a Free Report on "Black Belt Entrepreneur Secrets for Multiple Streams of Income," visit www.StephenWhittier.com.

About Stephen

Stephen Whittier is a lifelong educator and success coach with a real passion for helping others reach their personal and professional goals.

After graduating from Wheaton College at the top of his class, Stephen entered the public sector as a junior advertising account executive and copywriter. He returned to graduate school at Tufts University, where he also taught for more than four years before transitioning into a full-time entrepreneur and business owner.

Stephen built a multiple award-winning martial arts and fitness academy in Massachusetts, and is also the principal of Whittier International, specializing in online marketing and coaching for entrepreneurs in any field. By combining his many years of teaching with hands-on experience in best business practices and direct response marketing, Stephen has been able to develop a unique and effective approach to helping entrepreneurs take their businesses to the next level.

CHAPTER 6

What Wayne Gretzky, Sam Walton and a Werewolf Taught Me About Success

By Tim Keck

I used to be a cop. In fact, for over two decades, I was a gun-toting, badge-wearing, handcuff-carrying, crime fighter. And I loved it. Most of it at least. I even remember driving around one day, a few weeks into my career, thinking, "Wow. I'm actually getting *paid* to do this!"

It wasn't just the part about chasing bad guys that made police work so cool. It was also about all the interesting characters I got to meet. Whether co-workers, suspects or celebrities, I tried to learn something from each of the amazing people I met throughout my career. Now, for the first time, so can you!

WAYNE GRETZKY: THE GREAT ONE

It was a beautiful mid-summer day in northwest Arkansas, at one of the state's premier golf courses. The occasion was the Greg Norman Challenge, where the golf pro would match his skills against a trio of athletes from other sports.

My job was VIP protection. As the supervisor, I also got to decide which of the competitors I'd spend most of my time with and which ones would be assigned to other officers. While Greg Norman, Larry Bird and Ivan Lendl are all great athletes, Gretzky was already an icon, which made him an easy choice.

They don't call him "The Great One" for nothing. Wayne Gretzky holds 61 National Hockey League records and led his team to win the Stanley Cup four times. I'd heard he was an absolute gentleman and found that to be completely accurate. This was going to be great! A chance to learn about golf from a living legend. A hockey legend, true, but how much harder could golf be?

A *lot* harder evidently.

In hockey, Gretzky is a demi-god. But I watched him play golf like a mere mortal. The complete command of the game he played on ice failed to translate to the links. Like Bird and Lendl, the word "Mulligan!" came out of his mouth more than once. Wayne Gretzky, it turned out, was not a great golfer.

After shanking what could have been an easy shot, Gretzky walked back over to where I was standing with a disgusted look on his face. "Ouch," I said. "That's why I play hockey for a living," came the reply, accompanied by a sly grin.

That started me thinking. Here was a world-class athlete at the top of his game—a game arguably more difficult than golf. Both involve massive amounts of practice and concentration. So why wasn't Gretzky just as good at golf as he was at hockey?

For the same reason Michael Jordon isn't a baseball star.

Wayne Gretzky was born to play hockey. True, he's a naturally gifted athlete by any measure, but his talents and abilities come together perfectly on the ice. As the captain of a professional hockey team, he was doing exactly what he was *born* to do. And doing it extremely well.

Since then I have come to believe (and research bears this out) that each of us can do something at a world-class level. We can't be world-class at *anything*, but we can at *something*.

The key is to read some books on the topic or hire a personal coach and figure out what that thing is.

My time with Gretzky taught me that no one can be a star in every sport or every career. Trying to do so is a recipe for mediocrity. On the other hand, we can all become a "great one" at one thing. We just have to believe in ourselves, be open-minded, and do the hard work it takes to discover what we were created to do.

SAM WALTON: THE GAZILLIONAIRE

I got my start in law enforcement at the Bentonville, Arkansas, police department way back in 1979. After less than two weeks of training, in what had to be a monumental lack of judgement, they turned me loose on the poor citizens of Bentonville with a badge, some handcuffs, and a loaded gun. It's a wonder any of us survived.

Several months into my tenure I was running radar down on southeast 8th street. I clocked an old pick-up truck doing about 12 miles an hour over the limit. I stopped the vehicle and eased up to the driver's door using that sideways walk that everyone hates to see in their side-view mirror. Pausing just behind the door, I looked to make sure this fellow didn't have a gun. He didn't. Instead he was working to get his license out of his wallet. I greeted him professionally and asked for his identification. He craned to look over his left shoulder, handing it to me.

It wasn't until I saw the name, Samuel Moore Walton, that I realized just whom I'd stopped.

"Do you know why I stopped you sir?"

"Was I speeding?"

"Yes sir, you were doing 12 miles over the limit."

"Oh, I'm sorry. Just in a hurry, I guess."

"Wait here, sir. I will be right back."

Returning to my patrol car I was faced with a dilemma: Should I write a ticket to the most influential man in town? My first thought was not to write it, because I rarely ticketed anyone running only 12 over. Then it occurred to me that, by not issuing the ticket, I might be perceived as showing favoritism to someone because they were rich and powerful. On the other hand, having been the guy who cited the wealthiest man in America might move me toward folk hero status among my fellow officers. Hmmmmm.

"Mr. Walton, here is your license."

"Thank you."

"I am giving you a warning today, sir. Just slow down a bit, please."

"Thank you officer."

"You're welcome, sir. Have a nice day."

"You too, sir."

So I didn't write Sam Walton a ticket because I thought he should be treated like everyone else. So did he. I know this because later one of the rookies I'd trained stopped Mr. Walton on the same road for the same thing. (In all fairness, it was the street that ran in front of Walmart headquarters.) His interaction with Sam went something like this:

"Mr. Walton?"

"Yes."

"Sam Walton?"

"Yes, officer."

"You're Sam Walton…"

"Yes, sir."

"Uhhhhhhh….."

"Do your job son. Write me a ticket."

"Okay."

Mr. Walton then got a ticket for speeding. It was a citation he deserved, and he accepted it without complaint. Then he paid the fine like everyone else.

Shortly after that I left Bentonville PD, but I would still have occasion to encounter Sam, his wife Helen, and their children. If I only had one word to describe them, it would be "humble." And that's the success principle I learned from Mr. Sam. Humility is one of the keys to finding success, enjoying success and, most important, staying successful. In spite of building the world's biggest business from scratch and achieving a net worth of roughly a gazillion dollars, he never saw himself as better that others. He just wanted to be treated like everyone else. Maybe that's why he went out on top.

DOUG: THE WEREWOLF

He stood before me that night, staring intently into my eyes. His muscular body was blanketed in thick reddish hair, covered only by a pair of cut-off jean shorts. His torso was smeared with blood, and it dripped from his hands. Only one thought went through my mind: They didn't cover this at the police academy.

I was the swing-shift supervisor at the Rogers, Arkansas, police department that warm summer night when the call came in about a disturbance down on Glenwood Avenue. I arrived on the scene along with one of the best officers on my shift, Ted. As we approached the house, three sweaty guys came running across the lawn toward us. All were wide-eyed with fear and started excitedly telling us the story.

It seems that their friend was drunk and high, and he'd suddenly "lost it" and become violent. They went on to describe how the three of them tried to control him but couldn't. He was too strong for them.

Great. Three guys couldn't hold him down.

They called us because he attacked a full-length mirror, breaking it into a million pieces. Then he went through the entire house, punching or kicking every window. They warned us there were shards of glass everywhere and that their friend was bleeding profusely. They thought he might die.

I thought *we* might die.

We searched the little cottage, but all was quiet. Initiating a sweep of the woods out back, we soon heard unintelligible shouting coming from the house. My partner, Ted, and I snuck in through the back porch as we could hear the suspect moving around the kitchen. When I peeked around the corner to get a glimpse of this guy I couldn't believe what I saw. Nearly naked, covered in hair, soaked in blood. He looked like a werewolf.

And there I was without a single silver bullet.

I started talking softly to this fellow to try and calm him down, but he wasn't interested. To intimidate us, he smashed a big stereo into small plastic pieces, then flipped a large oak dining table onto its top with one fell swoop. It was apparent that a painful physical intervention would be necessary. I told Ted to cover me and, if this dude tried to bite me, to shoot him!

Ted drew his gun, and I stepped into the room with the werewolf.

As I moved toward him he would back away, always maintaining that piercing eye contact. We slowly circled the inverted table until he came to the kitchen sink where a number of dishes were drying on the rack. Unexpectedly, he picked up a plate and threw it at me like a Frisbee. I ducked, and it crashed into the wall behind me. Then he grabbed another and another, slinging them my direction as I dodged. Plates and saucers were exploding onto the ceiling and shattering on the floor. The scene was almost comical, until he ran out of plates and I noticed the only remaining items left in the drainer were cast iron skillets. I had to get to him before he grabbed one of those and tried to dent my skull with it.

I knew if he attacked with something so heavy and potentially deadly, Ted would have to shoot him to protect me. There had to be *something* I could do. We didn't have Tasers, and he was just too bloody and sweaty to grab on to. There was one thing that might work, but I'd never actually done it before. On the outside of the human thigh, about 6 inches above the knee, is a nerve motor point. When struck properly, this motor point shuts down the entire leg, taking even a werewolf out of the fight, but resulting in no permanent injury.

Grabbing my flashlight from its holder I walked quickly across the room toward the lycan. He grudgingly retreated from the sink and backed into the corner. Knowing I'd only have one shot at this, I stepped to the side and drew back for a big strike. Then I noticed that my target was mostly blocked by the cabinet he was crouching against—too late now.

I hit him as hard as I could as close to the motor point as possible, then jumped back into ready position—just in case. At that moment, it was as if time stopped. There was no noise or motion. I looked at him, and he looked at me, and there was a long pause. Then, very calmly, came this question: "What did you hit me with?"

Totally taken aback by the irony, I blinked twice and answered honestly, "my flashlight," bracing for the attack. He took one step toward me and fell to the floor. The technique had worked! His left leg was completely limp! Ted ran in and we quickly handcuffed our former foe, transporting him first to the hospital for an examination, then to jail.

So what's the lesson, you ask?

When trying to succeed, you'll undoubtedly encounter obstacles. Some will be particularly difficult to manage, and maybe even dangerous, causing you to doubt your next move. In times like this there will always be one thing that comes to mind. All your years of experience and education will come together and thrust an idea into your consciousness. The one thing will be an action you must take right now. During those critical times you must *do* that thing. Commit to it fully and follow through with gusto.

That's what helped me succeed in defanging a werewolf, and it's a concept that will help you, too. It's especially handy if you don't have a silver bullet.

Want to succeed at work and in life? Learn something from everyone you meet. Like Gretzky, do what you were meant to do and you will do it well. No matter what heights you reach, be as humble as Sam Walton, to insure you don't suffer a painful fall. And when things are tough, do that one thing you know you should do, even if it's hard. Then watch every bloody barrier start to fall.

Live these lessons, find success, and share your best with the world.

About Tim

Tim D. Keck, a veteran of two decades of crime-fighting, retired from law enforcement as chief of police. He has taken what he learned about thriving in a high-stress, high-stakes profession and brought those lessons to the world of work. The results have been phenomenal.

Tim is an author, speaker and coach who uses true stories and improvisational humor to engage audiences at all levels. He has been quoted in publications from *Newsweek* to *The New York Times* and has made several appearances on national television.

Tim's *Bulletproof Teams* framework is a formula for success under stress. It's helping organizations develop strong teams composed of passionate people who love their jobs *and* the people they work with, ensuring a maximum performance culture.

He has assisted organizations from Los Angeles to London and from Calgary to the Caymans. Clients include Kimberly-Clark, Wal-Mart Stores, Tyson Foods, PepsiCo, Marriott, Arvest Bank Group, Apex Tool Group, J.B. Hunt, Pratt & Whitney, Total Oil – Canada, and many more.

While Tim now serves as managing partner at Performance Insights, LLC (a boutique management consultancy based in northwest Arkansas), he has long been recognized as an innovative and successful leader both inside and outside of the law enforcement profession.

During his police career, Chief Keck worked his way up through the ranks, serving in many capacities, including patrol officer, K-9 trainer, detective supervisor and SWAT team commander. He has testified before a congressional committee, provided VIP protection to celebrities, and spearheaded a multinational undercover investigation.

Chief Keck's work has also been recognized by several federal agencies, including the Drug Enforcement Agency and Department of Homeland Security. The Department of Justice wrote "The FBI and the American people have been the beneficiaries of your professionalism and dedication to duty…" about his career-long efforts.

For more information, please visit www.performanceinsights.net or www.bulletproofteams.com.

You may contact Tim directly at (479) 644-1717 or tim@performanceinsights.net.

CHAPTER 7

From Great to "Good Enough": How to Turn Your Success Into Fulfillment

By Dr. Timothy Benson

I'll never forget the day I first sat in the therapist's office. As a part of our psychiatry residency training and for our overall well-being it was "highly recommended" that we participate in our own therapy. This was also said to be an important exercise for us to better understand the patient's perspective. Not wanting to be the only one in my class to abstain, I reluctantly agreed to engage.

My heart raced as I pondered who would see me there in the basement waiting room of the therapist's home office. As I nervously thumbed through an outdated *Better Homes and Gardens* magazine (wishing it were *Sports Illustrated*), I experienced a mixed wave of anxiety, fear and anger. I thought to myself, "Was this really a part of the training, or was this my training director's subtle way of saying I needed help." My mind was now off to the races. "I can't believe they tricked me and I fell for it. I should leave right now."

At that moment, the office door opened, and the client before me walked out. I immediately buried my head in the magazine so I wouldn't be recognized. I then heard my name called, "Dr. Benson?" I thought to myself, "Great, she just had to say my name out loud." I looked up and saw a petite, middle-aged Caucasian female waving for me to enter the room. It didn't matter that she had an inviting smile and warm eyes, I wasn't happy to be there, and I was going to let her know it. I sat down across from her in an old-cloth lounge chair. Her office was scattered with books and papers. Without hesitation, I began, "I'm going to be honest with you; I'm only here because I'm being forced to be here (that was a lie). Besides, there's absolutely nothing you can tell me about what it means to be an African-American man trying to compete in a stressful and sometimes hostile academic environment." She sat, quietly. With my best look of disdain, I finished what I had to say, wanting so earnestly for her to understand that the very notion anyone would suggest that I, of all people, needed help, was ludicrous. When finished, I was surprised about how pleased I was with myself for having decimated this complete stranger.

Unfazed, she waited to ensure I was done. She then gave me "the look." It was a look of compassion that was oddly familiar. It was the same validating and reassuring look my mom would give me when I was a kid, right before I would burst into tears and run into her arms. In a calm voice she asked, "So how are you really doing?" And that's all it took. The flood gates opened, and I let it all out. I began talking about feeling overwhelmed with always having to prove myself and how I felt no one understood or cared about how much pressure I was under. And despite winning many national awards and being accepted to one of the nation's top psychiatry programs at Harvard, my fear of failing and letting my family and supporters down was a constant struggle. The list went on and on. It was all a blur. The next thing I remember was her saying, "Well, our time is up." Startled as if I had been jolted from a trance, I replied, "What do you mean our time is up? I have so much more to say!" Needless to say, every week for years, I continued talking (for "educational" purposes, of course).

The importance of that experience cannot be overstated. What was revealed to me was that in the pursuit of success I had overcome many barriers, but somehow now I had become my biggest obstacle to progress. I had learned how to climb the mountaintop but didn't know I needed to bring oxygen in order to survive there. Caught off-guard and my confidence shaken, I had begun to question everything, especially why I was even on this road in the first place. To my surprise I wasn't alone. In my 10 years of working with high achievers in the field of athletics, entertainment and business, I learned the truth about the pursuit of success. It comes with a price. There are the costs we anticipate, but the most devastating ones are those we don't expect. More important, on this journey I learned that the greatest challenge isn't always in the acquisition of new skills or knowledge but rather in the letting go of the "baggage" accumulated along the way.

THE ORIGINS OF "SUCCESS STRESS"

Whether you're a doctor or a professional athlete, success brings universal changes to your life. Whether a Hollywood celebrity or a corporate CEO, managing the impact of your performance is a constant challenge. Unfortunately, society prepares us very little for these struggles, and with a limited view of what success might be, we stumble in the darkness trying to find our way.

For us to move in the right direction, we must first shed some light on what success truly means. That includes not only the positive stereotypes we've come to know but also the negative and less appealing aspects. Without question, this idea of success is inextricably woven through the fabric of the American dream. Thousands of books have been dedicated to describing what it takes to become successful. However, there's little that's written about what to do when you arrive and how to deal with the inner challenges that are experienced underneath the veneer of achievement.

Competition breeds secrecy. As much as we want to be recognized for our accomplishments, the flip side is to withhold all of what it took to get there. Somewhat like the baker who will give you the recipe to her prize-winning cake but neglects to include the key ingredient that makes it special. Consequently, the public is often left with marveling the fruits of your success yet not privy to the true cost of it.

Nevertheless, step by step we climb the mountain until one day we reach the peak. Satisfied with our accomplishment, we try to set up our camp and enjoy the view. But in reality, success isn't like this. Upon our arrival to the mountain peak, we then see several other mountains and peaks that require us to continue climbing. With success comes increasing demands, pressures and responsibilities. Unless we're prepared for these challenges, we may develop dysfunctional ways of handling the success we've achieved. As a result, we may take missteps and eventually fall down the mountain that took us so much effort to climb in the first place.

We don't have to look far to see examples of this. In the media there are constant reports of celebrities in business, sports and politics who have seemingly "fallen from grace." More often than not, their fall can be attributed to a combination of several common dysfunctional factors.

5 COMMON BARRIERS TO HEALTHY SUCCESS

1. *Limited definitions:* How you define success has the potential to shape how you pursue it and experience it. Our definitions can derive from our own experience and desires or through the experiences or expectations of others. Definitions of success forged from outside of one's own values is likely to lead to resentment. Definitions based on constantly fluctuating variables provides for a fragile foundation. Self-worth will rise and fall with the next victory or loss, the next positive regard or negative criticism. This emotional roller coaster often leads individuals staggering to find a solid sense of self outside of their accomplishments or titles.

2. *Distortions:* In any environment adaptation is required for survival. Just like the body attempts to constantly achieve homeostasis, the mind continually adapts by making meaning of stimuli we're exposed to. Along the often lonely road of achievement the view of the world begins to change as environmental conditions change. As Oliver William Holmes notes, "A mind stretched by a new experience can never go back to its old dimensions." Many high achievers are thrust into a different world with new ways of communicating and new cultural norms. The challenge lies in understanding and negotiating norms and values of both the culture of origin and the culture of competition. What's accepted in one may be abhorred or even illegal in the other. The failure to recognize and manage these discrepancies can have drastic consequences.

3. *Dependence:* Dependence plays a complex role in the quest for success. In fact, there's a constant battle between interdependence and counterdependence. No one achieves success in isolation. When and whom to rely on throughout this journey becomes a critical skill. Dependence can manifest as emotional attachments to people, behaviors, substances or fame itself. An over-reliance on anything can place one in a vulnerable position, making it easier to be manipulated or exercise poor judgment.

4. Doubt: Behind closed doors many successful individuals will admit to doubt being a constant companion. No matter what level you reach, there will always exist some level of it. In fact, doubt and fear are often intertwined and must be managed adequately in order to succeed. However, when doubt begins to erode your ability to trust yourself or others, personal interactions and healthy interpretations become more difficult. A good example of this was examined in the studies on "The Impostor Syndrome." Successful individuals, despite their vast accomplishments, struggle with the fear of being "found out." This and other forms of self-doubt stifles growth and can lead to feeling perpetually unfulfilled.

5. Disappointment: "Is this it?" is a common question that occurs when a long-awaited dream is accomplished. The inspiring fantasy abruptly becomes a painful reality. As the excitement of the dream achieved fades, we're left with the mundane reality of new responsibilities and increased demands. Invariably we'll all be disappointed in one fashion or another. For the high achiever, the letdown can be significant. The disappointment can change one's view of the world, alter future aspirations, and create tentativeness in one's willingness to take risks.

So how do you manage "success stress" and go beyond the aforementioned barriers? Throughout the years I've taught many concepts that help to generate a greater sense of fulfillment. In my private coaching programs, clients report that learning how to "strategically let go," "build a personal board of directors," "compete without comparing," and many other concepts have proved to be extremely helpful. However, in both my personal and professional experience, there has been no other concept that has been more liberating for the successful high achiever than that of embracing "good enough."

EMBRACING "GOOD ENOUGH"

In the psychology literature, there's much that's written on the "good enough" parent. In brief, the concept was born out of studies on early childhood development. What was discovered was that parents, more specifically the mother, didn't need to be perfect or exceptional in order to successfully raise a healthy child. She just needed to be "good enough" at meeting the basic physical and emotional needs of the child. This same concept can be applied to both our personal and professional worlds. The culture of competition conditions us to believe that we have to always be better and show no weakness. Otherwise, we'll lose. So it is the constant drive of always wanting and striving for more that causes us to never feel settled or satisfied. "Good enough" in this context doesn't refer to giving up or lowering your standards. Rather, it's about developing a healthy self-acceptance. It's about being OK with who you are (strengths and limitations) and appreciating what you've accomplished. At the end of the day, it's the realization that your circumstances don't control your life—you do.

I often pose the question to my clients, "If you were to leave the earth today, would the world keep moving on?" Of course, we all inherently know that life on earth would continue, but the distortions of success tend to make us believe that the world we created would collapse without us. As a result, we tend to give in to the pull of being everything to everybody, leaving little to no room for our own needs.

For many of those who are on the fast track of life, the thought of accepting this concept may feel like taking your foot off the gas pedal. However, it's much more like psychologically shifting gears so your engine doesn't explode. The irony of embracing "good enough" is it often leads to greater and more fulfilling results. When you're freed from self-imposed, limited psychological constructs, space is created for new growth and greater mental efficiency. The "good enough" principle helps to give you permission to say no without fearing that relationships will be permanently damaged. It helps you reconcile your limitations and allows you the ability to step out of the exhausting pull of constantly proving your worthiness. Finally, embracing "good enough" allows you the permission to "stay in your lane." You're more able to construct a life that emanates from your passion, that place where your confidence and competence feed off each other, drawing out your best self.

In summary, whether you've already scaled the mountain or have just started on the path toward your next level of success, you'll be challenged in learning how to experience success in terms of growth rather than a specific outcome. Best isn't always better. And although time and energy prohibits us from being everything we are capable of becoming, I firmly believe there's more than enough room to be more accepting and appreciative of who we already are. And that my friends is not only "great" for you to know, but more important, "good enough" for you to grow.

About Dr. Benson

Dr. Timothy Benson is a Clinical Instructor in Psychiatry at Harvard Medical School and Founder and CEO of Gamewise Consulting LLC, a company that provides strategic support for elite performers and their families. Often referred to as "The Success Psychiatrist," Dr. Benson's motto is "Helping the Best Get Better." Having been a member of Harvard's clinical faculty for almost a decade, he has successfully used "strength-based approaches" to engage and empower professionals who work in high-stress environments.

In addition to his coaching programs for athletes, entertainers and entrepreneurs, Dr. Benson speaks nationally on the topics of "Outperforming Yourself", "Succeeding Against the Odds" and "Surviving Success: Preventing Your Dream From Becoming a Disaster." He has also been an invited panelist at Harvard Business School and Wharton School of Business to address the psychological dynamics of being the "first in the family" to reach certain social, economic and educational milestones.

To learn more about Dr. Tim Benson, "The Success Psychiatrist," please visit www. drtimothybenson.com or visit www.gamewiseconsulting.com.

CHAPTER 8

18 Tips for Staying Lean and Fit While Traveling

By an Uberbusy Road Warrior,
Anastasia Chopelas, Ph.D.

Shortly after I turned 40, my health took a rapid downward dive, despite regular exercise and healthy eating. My blood pressure was through the roof, my cholesterol was up, and I had a case of very painful arthritis. My weight also ballooned by 50 pounds after menopause: I was 50, fat and frumpy. This was a shock since I was lean all my life. With no energy, a lot of pain and a foggy brain, I was unable to function well.

Since I'm a research scientist, I did what comes naturally: I thoroughly researched what caused these problems and found solutions without medication. This included tightening my exercise and nutrition program as well as increasing meal frequency to keep my mind alert. During the 1990s, flying across the Atlantic several times a year forced me to pick up, develop and practice habits that would maintain health and avoid the typical meeting/conference health booby traps.

This chapter is inspired by the many road warriors I've spoken to who tell me that their health routines go out the window while on the road. They typically gain weight and lose fitness while traveling. One businesswoman I spoke to said she has regained 22 of the 45 pounds she lost the previous year in less than six months of traveling. Her business requires her to be in front of a video camera often, which means she's not presenting her best self.

Since we, as businesspeople, need to be in top shape mentally and physically to deliver our best service, even while traveling, a sedentary lifestyle of too much drink and the wrong food is self-defeating. Good physical health means your mind is clear, and you can do your best thinking, negotiating, speech delivery, seminars and socializing. Taking good care of yourself gives you that extra edge.

The first and major step that needs to be taken is making the decision that this is a priority. *And it is!* Once you've made the decision, following these tips are easy.

First, as a rule, travel usually brings out the parade of carbohydrate, sugar, and fat-laden "food"/snacks. As tempting and as tasty as these are, stop thinking about them; stop looking at them. They're not good options, ever, period. They fog your brain, make you feel sleepy and bloat you up so your pants don't fit in short order. I, for one, am distracted when my pants get tight. Healthier options for each venue are given below.

Preparation before travel:

1. **Plan ahead for your exercise.** If attending a conference, find the schedule and start your planning. Decide what time you're going to exercise, and stick to it *as if it were a doctor's appointment.* Keep it no matter what, and not just when you feel like it. When a meeting is set at 7 am, get up at 5 to 5:30 a.m. to exercise. No excuse is good enough to skip it.

2. **Find facilities ahead of time**. Check if your hotel has a gym or, if you belong to a national chain such as 24-Hour Fitness, if one is nearby. If not, check if there are other gyms nearby. You can often buy or get guest passes for a week at a time to various gyms.

3. **If no gym is at hand, exercise in your room or outdoors.** Take running/walking shoes and exercise clothes. You can take a brisk walk, run or do intervals outdoors if the weather permits. If not, take minimal hotel room exercise equipment with you such as exercise bands, a DVD or iPod with music/workout, and/or P90X bands. If you have a subscription service, such as Netflix, you can find exercise programs to follow there. The standbys of sit-ups and push-ups work quite well to get your heart pumping. Try mountain climbers,

burpees, and Spiderman pushups or other whole-body exercises. Do at least three sets of each. You'll definitely feel great and ready to roll afterwards.

4. **If you're traveling by car, consider taking a cooler** full of healthy foods, including fruits, vegetables and precooked protein. Cook up several meals in advance and put them in separate plastic containers. Hotels all have either fridges or ice dispensers to keep it cool on location. Many have microwaves. I've even taken a small camping kit with plates, a pan, and some forks and my small portable camping stove. It saves a lot of time to eat breakfast in your room, and you get exactly what you need in the morning in nothing flat. (It takes less than 10 minutes to fry eggs and potatoes, eat and clean up!)

5. **If you're traveling internationally or far, pack healthy staples.** Packets of tuna in foil pouches (now sold everywhere), packets of protein powder (a plastic shaker cup helps here), meal replacement bars (watch for too much sugar or grains), dried fruit, nuts like raw almonds or walnuts. When I traveled from Germany to the United States several times a year, I would take a few things, including a couple of meals for on the plane, then scout out the local grocery stores and stock up on portable foods. This included low-fat cheese sticks, roasted chicken from delis, fruit, packaged salads, beef jerky, etc.

6. **If you're going through several time zones and you have trouble sleeping, try melatonin to regulate your sleep cycle.** Rest while jet-lagged is paramount to feeling clear headed and energetic.

On the road:
7. **Stay hydrated during travel.** Airplane and even car travel wreak havoc on the water balance and regularity of our body cycles. Getting plenty of water helps counteract this problem. Don't overdo the coffee: Stick to one or two cups a day. Keeping caffeine consumption down also helps with jet lag. Keep a bottle of water with you at all times, especially

during long sessions of a meeting or conference. Good hydration promotes good sleep, and a clear head and minimizes hunger.

8. **Get enough sleep.** It's tempting to close out parties. They're fun. I've done it. But without enough sleep, the planned exercise is tougher, and the brain fogs up very quickly. Instead stay connected with the people you meet via phone or email. It will make the relationship lasting and more beneficial.

9. **Mini-mart shopping for car travel.** If you're traveling by car and have opted to *not* take a cooler, there are many things in mini-marts that are healthy options: low-fat cheese sticks, cottage cheese, salads, fruit, even dried fruit and nuts (watch these, they're high in calories, and raw is better, but roasted will do in a pinch). Avoid chips, crackers (high in fat), candy, soda, alcohol, even diet soda. Better to get a flavored water, tea or coffee. Many mini-marts have fast-food joints inside. Subway allows you to get low-fat meals and salads. These are a poor semblance to real food but are somewhat nourishing and better than pizza or deep-fried chicken.

10. **Don't overdo the alcohol.** Almost everyone enjoys their wine or favorite drink, but stick to one and then drink soda water with a twist of lemon or lime. Alcohol has a lot of empty calories and affects your brain adversely. You'll also have a clearer head in the morning and won't get so dehydrated, one of the banes of travel.

11. **If traveling by plane, don't eat the airplane food unless you're traveling business or first class.** There the food is almost edible. The best bet is to pack a lunch at home, although the continually changing TSA regulations make it hard to keep up with what's allowable. Because the carbohydrate, salt and sugar-laden foods airplanes serve make you so sleepy, getting anything done during the flight becomes near impossible. Instead find something in the airport shops/food malls: My one regular buy is a bottle of water, and if desperate to eat, a fruit and whatever protein I can find, and/or fruit-nut mixes. You can find fresh fruit,

salads and healthy snacks at some of the stands. I know pizza or tempura looks and tastes good, heck I like it too, but restrict that to a once-a-week treat. Better choices can be found at Mexican stands (eschew the deep-fried shells and choose warmed-up corn tortillas instead)

12. **If driving more than three hours, take bathroom breaks where you can walk around, eat a good snack/meal, and refresh yourself.** You'll arrive fresher and ready to work at the other end.

13. **On the day of travel, exercise early in the day.** You won't feel so restless during a long travel day, plus it helps you rest later in the day by promoting a good night's sleep.

Upon arrival and during your stay:
14. **Unless you absolutely have to get to a meeting immediately, settle in to your room to unwind and rest.** Take a walk outside to clear your head, if possible. Too much rushing around means you'll get tired and start making bad choices. The subconscious starts demanding energy, which we interpret as hunger, even if we're just tired. This is another reason to stay hydrated, since we get the same sort of signal to eat even if we're just thirsty. Staying well rested, hydrated and fresh helps us maintain the resolve to practice good health habits while traveling.

15. **If you didn't bring your food, scout out the local grocery stores and stock up on portable foods.** This includes low-fat cheese sticks, roasted chicken from delis, fruit, packaged salads, etc.

16. **Use the 80 percent rule for treats.** This means eat healthy 80 percent of the time, and indulge in your favorites 20 percent of the time. This means out of 21 meals a week, you can eat something extra for four meals out of the week, like a dessert or piece of pizza instead of the chicken salad. We can't possibly stick to a stringent plan 100 percent of the time. Besides, our metabolism needs a revving up from time to time, and this does it and does it well. Mind you, this isn't a pig-out, just a treat with extra calories.

17. **At restaurants, choose the lighter choices.** Give the breadbasket back to the waiter. Choose fish or chicken over steak. Get salads without croutons (they're very fatty) and dressing on the side, or better oil and vinegar. Other dangerous ingredients in salads are luncheon meats and gobs of cheese. Good choices are all vegetables, boiled eggs, a few nuts or seeds (but only a teaspoonful), a spoonful of parmesan, a few raisins or other fruit, or roasted chicken. All restaurants will accommodate lighter food choices. Ask the waiter/waitress! Substitute vegetables for French fries. Take your baked potato with condiments on the side. Divide down the potato to a small side and toss the rest into the foil. Divide a large meal immediately upon being served and ask for a doggie bag. It's less tempting to eat too much when it's not in plain view. Take it with you for lunch the next day.

18. **At conferences when breaks aren't forthcoming, take in snacks and meals.** Never let the conference timing dictate when you're going to eat. For example, I eat every three hours because it keeps my energy and metabolism up and helps tremendously with brain fatigue. Snacks to take in: fruit, raw nuts, meal substitution bars, and even a meal packed up in a plastic container. Try bringing a couple of empty containers from home with plastic utensils for packing up food and eating during breaks, or you can buy containers on site and toss them when done.

You don't have to do everything—try a tip or two, work it in. Next time, work in another tip. Eventually, you'll find you arrive back home in as good shape as you left, or perhaps even better!

About Anastasia

Anastasia has been an internationally active research scientist and professor for nearly 40 years. Her 50-plus original research articles and book chapters appear in top journals and periodicals that are housed in libraries all over the world. Armed with her doctorate in chemistry and her research experience, she solved several of her own health crises without resorting to side-effect-laden medication.

After wading through the plethora of anecdotal evidence and misinformation, she found that much of the advice is ineffectual. Getting to the truth required reading original reports and testing first herself and then reporting this to others, many of who also got the relief they needed. The methods work. She originally reported the results in a series of articles and has now written her first books: *Get Rid of Bad Cholesterol, Get Rid of Bad Cholesterol Guide,* and *50 Tips for Getting* and *Staying Healthy While Super Busy.*

Her health program is a holistic, five-step plan, including more than just diet but also lifestyle habits that are powerful for promoting good health, from youth to middle age to retirement and beyond. The program serves to not only lower cholesterol but also helps lower blood pressure, burn off body fat, improve brain function, and improve overall health and vitality. She teaches you how to take control of your health without spending all day cooking or exercising. She lives the plan, fitting it into her full and busy life, both at home and while on the road.

Prof. Chopelas received her MS from Caltech and her Ph.D. from UCLA. She has worked in all venues for scientists, private industry, research institutes, universities, and is now owner of Embrace Your Vitality. She speaks two languages fluently: Greek from her heritage and German from her 13-year residence in Germany. She loves to draw, paint and take photographs. You'll find her artwork and photos on her websites www.embraceyourvitality.com and www.getridofbadcholesterol.com.

CHAPTER 9

6 Steps Away From Getting What You Want—Every Time!

By Dayan Douse, Ph.D.

Take your pick of your favorite reality television show, "House Wives" (any one), "Kim and Klohe Take New York," "The Bachelor," "The Apprentice" or "American Idol," and they all teach us some very important steps to achieving success that generally go unnoticed.

Did you know that eight months after debuting on "Britain's Got Talent," Susan Boyle went from church choir member to a bestselling multimillionaire singer. The Real Housewives of New York have all written books. Aaron McCargo Jr., winner of Season 4 of "The Next Food Network Star," is now spokesperson for the Great American Dine Out, a campaign to end childhood hunger.

At least 20 percent of the stories in *People Weekly, Star, In Touch, OK!*, and many other gossip magazines, entertainment TV shows, and celebrity websites are about reality TV show stars.

In each show, all the reality stars have something in common—they all are facing some very ugly truths, some uglier than others. Many feel guilt throughout their journey (probably for some of the stunts they've pulled). However, they all eventually take personal responsibility for their own success and come to a point of declaring what they truly want. They take action to get what they want and claim their wins when they get it. Success doesn't include laying blame on others, rationalizing your failures, or feeling shame for your current situation, which is where some of the reality stars remain stuck. But even if you despise the characters, the shenanigans they pull, or the success they've achieved, they all follow the same process for success—every time and now it's your turn.

Whether looking for success in your personal or professional life, each one of the top six steps to take personal responsibility for your success is important and repeatable. As you read through each step, there are principles you need to be aware of before you go any further. First, you must start with step one, every time; the steps are repeated in the same order whenever we accomplish a goal; you cannot skip steps; and you can stay stuck on any step for as long as you like, which is exactly what keeps you from accomplishing your goals and achieving success, so don't stay stuck!

STEP 1: CONFRONT THE UGLY TRUTH

Determine what's standing in your way. You may not want to hear this, but the ugly truth is you are standing in the way of your own success, period. Sure, many external factors cause us to fail, hold us back, and get in our way, but you have the power and ability to change your circumstances; you simply have to face what's true about the situation. James Baldwin said it best: "Not everything that is faced can be changed. But nothing can be changed until it is faced."

While working with an organization on ways to improve their performance management process, I came across an individual who had received poor performance appraisals for many years; I know what you're thinking—why was he still there? That's a chapter in my next book, *Let Go: Leaders Who Take Responsibility for Developing High Performing Teams*. I decided to sit with him to discuss his performance, and just as I thought, he blamed his manager, the organization, and his girlfriend for his poor performance. I began teaching him the top six steps to take personal responsibility for your success and soon the conversations began to change. As our conversations went on, he began facing some ugly truths; he simply needed to own his performance and stop putting it on everything and everyone else. That was in 2004; he still works for the same company, and since that time, he has received nothing but positive performance appraisals.

Many companies needed to face some ugly truths as well, like GM, Chrysler and Exxon, to name a recent few. Perhaps your organization needs to face some ugly truths.

We can easily find others to blame for our rut, even when it's not readily apparent who's responsible. Before long, the blame game gets old, and we begin trying to find reasonable justifications and telling ourselves logical stories for why we're not getting what we want. It's not until we face the truth (I fear failure or sometimes, even success; haven't done my best; don't have the skills, or need to choose something different) that we begin taking personal responsibility for our success. Success starts here, but oftentimes, ends here as well.

STEP 2: GET PAST GUILT

Stop feeling bad about what you discovered. Confronting the truth can be both difficult and rewarding. It's hard to consider that we would stand in our own way of success. When we do, we feel bad as a result, eventually recognizing that it's the choices we make, situations we create, and decisions we reach that often stand in the way of our success. This leads to feelings of shame and guilt. However, that's not the only time we feel guilty when trying to accomplish our toughest goals. Occasionally we can even feel guilt for our successes. Becoming more successful than your friends, colleagues and neighbors can lead to "survivor guilt," referring to the belief that fate has treated you better than others in your life, or that your favorable treatment was at someone else's expense.

A few years ago, two friends working for one of my largest clients found themselves faced with this very situation. One friend wanted the other's position—wow! This could have been a difficult situation to confront, so we set down to talk over the options. The friend who wanted the other's position initially felt shame for wanting what his good friend had worked so hard to achieve. Feeling he was more qualified for the job, he wrestled with how to approach the situation. Should he tell him he wanted his job, go after other positions he was equally qualified for, or grumble to the leaders in the organization that he was better suited for the job, hoping they would make the change?

The choice he would make took courage and the ability to explore the truth about what he wanted and get past the guilt. He made the choice to go directly to his friend and tell him what he wanted and his plans for getting it. That's courage! Surprisingly, the friend who held the position never batted an eye, instead asking how they might work together so they both could get exactly what they wanted. It turned out that he got the position, and his friend moved on to explore other opportunities within the company that he never envisioned, successfully facing many of his own ugly truths.

The simplest way to get past guilt and shame starts with being aware and clear about your intentions. If your intentions are focused on you and not directed toward changing others, then you'll avoid prolonged periods of guilt and shame.

Whether you feel shame for the role you play in creating the hurdles that stand in your way or "survivor guilt," you must get past guilt to declaring what you really want in order to achieve success.

STEP 3: DECLARE WHAT YOU WANT

Be honest and open about what you want. Society would tell us that declaring what you want is selfish and boastful. Let's be clear: Declaring what you want doesn't mean you're going to get it! However, it does provide clarity for you and everyone else around you. It's not until you insist on getting what you want or foolishly feel entitled that you become selfish and boastful. Declaring what you want simply speaks to your desires, purpose and goals without guilt, shame or fear. The moment you honestly and openly declare what you want is the moment you begin working toward your success.

One of my clients' daughters loved the game of basketball and wanted badly to play for her school team. Everyone knew how competitive she was and that she merely wanted to be part of the team. Although she had spent many hours practicing, she didn't make the team. Heartbroken about the results of her tryout, she decided to do something out of the ordinary and play chess with the school chess club. What was interesting is she had never played chess before and no one in her family knew how to play either, but she simply loved to compete and wanted to be part of a team. Not even basketball could stand in the way of that. She learned the game of chess very quickly and found that she was very good—so good, that she would eventually become captain of that team, which placed fifteenth in the nation that year. Her desire to play basketball never left, and she would eventually play for her school and win a state title.

The first question I ask anyone who has a concern, worry, issue or problem is, What do you want? What's always surprising to me is that most people don't know. They can tell you what they want from others or about the symptoms of the problem, but declaring what you want is about you. It's not until you're clear and can declare what you want that you can take the necessary steps to becoming successful.

STEP 4: TAKE ACTION!

Go after what you want and fail fast. Now that you've confronted the truth, stopped feeling guilty for identifying your role in that truth, and know exactly what you want, it is time to move and take action! Taking personal responsibility for your success means going after your desires, purpose and goals with every intention of achieving success, every time! Jack Canfield advises us to take action even when we're not exactly sure what to do. The reason is with every action comes both successes and mistakes, and it's through our mistakes that we learn and grow. Failing fast in your actions is an important concept, which means taking some risks, being comfortable with making some mistakes so you can learn, course correct and proceed.

Oftentimes we'll overanalyze a situation, repeatedly seeking others' opinions (what should I do or what do you think?), even talking ourselves out of taking action (what if, or I'm not sure I can do it). Failing fast allows us to take action even when we're not exactly sure what to do, because we realize there's much more for us to gain in taking action, even if we fail, than it is to have "analysis paralysis" and do nothing.

While working with area schools to maximize student achievement and close the achievement gap, one of my daughters' close friends struggled with reading at her grade level, which affected her grades in all subjects. When the faculty noticed through assignments and tests that she was below reading level, they took action. They immediately notified the parents, provided them resources, and even spent time tutoring. With good intentions, her parents selected a few difficult books they felt would inspire their daughter. They quickly failed fast when they discovered that the harder books actually discouraged her. They began using different techniques (such as the five-finger rule) to select 'just right' books for their daughter and read with her nightly. Within six months her test scores had dramatically improved, and the next year she was not only reading at grade level but had achieved A's in every subject.

If you don't take action, you simply cope with your current situation and failure, and settle for something less than success. The concept is simple but not easy. Either take action or accept your situation!

STEP 5: CLAIM YOUR WINS

Celebrate the little successes. We often wait to celebrate our major successes: getting that job promotion, finishing the book you've been working on for years but can't find the time to complete because life keeps getting in the way, or finishing a project without defects, etc. We miss celebrating the journey, the breakthroughs, the discoveries. When working with teams, I often open meetings with asking who has a win to share, and oftentimes I get silence as people try to dig deep for the big thing that happened. My wife always reminds me to stop and smell the roses, to enjoy what you've accomplished before moving to the next big thing. If you overlook your success and quickly move on, you'll find yourself disappointed and frustrated with life for no reason.

A good friend of mine often tells a story of a time in his life when things felt a little gloomy for no apparent reason. He had a successful consulting practice, beautiful family and home. However, something just didn't feel right. When asked by his friend on their early-morning run, what was bothering him, he simply replied, I don't know. His friend asked, when was the last time you celebrated a win? He was puzzled and not sure what he was asking. The friend advised him that when you omit the smaller wins in life, your spirit grieves. He had accomplished so much but had not stopped long enough to notice.

We all succeed every day that we are pursuing our goals. Yet most of us never acknowledge the thousands of things we do right, even when we make mistakes and haven't reached the finish line. When we acknowledge our own successes early and often, we build confidence, motivation, and commitment to stay the course during adversity. Remember, success breeds success.

STEP 6: BEGIN AGAIN

Look to continuously improve what you've accomplished. Overnight success is rare, but sustainable success, the kind that leads to great accomplishments, is created by working hard over time, patience, repeated practice, and continuous adjustments based on frequent feedback. To achieve cumulative gains, building win after win, you must take personal responsibility for your success.

- **Step 1: Confront the Ugly Truth:** Determine what's standing in your way.

- **Step 2: Get Past Guilt:** Stop feeling bad about what you discovered.

- **Step 3: Declare What You Want:** Be honest and open about what you want.

- **Step 4: Take Action!** Go after what you want and fail fast.

- **Step 5: Claim Your Wins:** Celebrate the little successes.

- **Step 6: Begin Again**

German writer Johann Wolfgang von Goethe said it best: what you get by achieving your goals is not as important as what you become by achieving your goals. Whether looking for success in your personal or professional life, each step to taking personal responsibility for your success is important and repeatable. As you read each step again, remember these principles:

- You must start with step one, every time.

- The steps are repeated in the same order whenever we accomplish a goal.

- You cannot skip steps.

- You can stay stuck on any step for as long as you like, which is exactly what keeps you from accomplishing your goals and achieving success, so don't stay stuck!

What you're about to become is confident in your power and ability to succeed—every time!

About Dayan

Dayan M. Douse, Ph.D., is the founder and president of P.R.I.D.E Consulting, a human behavior and development company committed to teaching simple, tested, repeatable processes and techniques, which help individuals, teams and organizations solve problems at the root and develop excellence in every pursuit. Services range from practical leader and employee development workshops, to individual and group mentoring and coaching, to keynote speaking.

Dayan has worked with the world's most outspoken, celebrated and successful advisors on personal and shared responsibility and is known for his work with individuals and teams on leadership development and personal and shared responsibility. He's committed to "Building People" in order to help them accomplish their toughest goals. He finds creative ways to urge individuals and teams to keep moving toward excellence.

Located in Michigan, P.R.I.D.E Consulting works in partnership with corporations, non-profit organizations, school systems, churches and criminal justice departments. To learn more about Dayan and how to accomplish your most challenging goals, visit www.pride-consulting.com, or call (248) 270-7879.

www.PRIDE-CONSULTING.com

CHAPTER 10

Your Life Is Calling: 10 Steps to Your Reinvention

By Donna Rippley

A very special joy in life is discovering your calling. I think people find their calling by giving themselves the gift of time to turn inward and think about their skills, talents, interests, values and accomplishments, then looking at the world of possibilities that connect all of those things. The place where there's an intersect of your skills, talents, interests, values and accomplishments creates a uniquely matched and meaningful calling for you. Once you find it, nothing will stop you.

When I figured out the world of coaching was where I wanted to be, it meant I needed to fill in some gaps in my background to coach at a professional level. I wanted to be on the cutting edge of what was happening in the coaching field. At the time, I was working as an administrator in the education field and wanting to study executive and business coaching from an international coaching school. That presented some logistical issues. One of the courses was a three-month seminar originating from New Zealand. The time difference created a good news-bad news scenario. The good news was that the course was being offered via teleconference at a time that wasn't during my workday so I could take the course. The bad news was it was from 2:30 a.m. to 4:00 a.m. My determination set in and I enrolled. I went to bed one night a week for 12 weeks at my regular time and set the alarm for 2 a.m. so I would be awake enough by the time the seminar started to be an active participate. I huddled in a blanket during the call in my pajamas and, if called on, coached business owners across the world! That's what I mean when I say once you find your calling, nothing will stop you! My biggest fear was that it would all catch up with me, and I would end up falling asleep during a class or missing my alarm. I'm happy to report many of my other courses involved travel in the United States and regular daylight hours. I used my vacation time to make those courses work.

Since those days long ago, I've had the privilege to journey with many clients as they embark on their own mission to discover their calling and reinvent their life. It has been an inspiration to share the reinvention process with them. One thing I've noticed is reinventions come in lots of different sizes. Some people make a small change almost like a tune-up to the life they're currently living while others make a big career/life change. I had one client attend a reinvention retreat, and the following Monday presented some changes to her supervisor about how her job responsibilities could be carried out differently to allow her to deliver a higher quality of support in a more timely manner to the organization. The changes included a different way of scheduling her days as well as some work from home days. It was a "win-win" situation, and the client feels like she's doing a better job for her company, doesn't commute as many days, and is now available at critical times rather than just scheduled times. Today, she feels rewarded and enjoys her professional life.

Another client was in a job that felt like exactly that, a job. It was a job that she was very successful at but not one that was her calling. Tracie took the job because she knew she had the skills that were required and the salary was good. After several years, she started to wonder if that was what she really wanted to keep doing. Tracie spent some time reflecting about what makes her uniquely her and what she's really passionate about. She knew it had to be something that had a strong connection to reading and helping people of all ages have great books and reading experiences. Tracie started looking at lots of different possibilities, and in the end decided she needed her master's degree to accomplish her new career plan. She developed a transition plan so she could keep working while she was moving toward her reinvention. Researching programs led her to a university that was offering a new degree in digital media. Tracie now has a map for her new plan and is halfway through her master's degree. She also changed jobs while she's going to school to add to her background in her newly selected field. Tracie is well on her way to a new career that she's very excited about.

Changes in the economy have been the catalyst for some people to change their career and seek a new calling. Paige was a successful building contractor until the economy changed that industry. Connecting some dots and combing her background knowledge, systems management, personality and "on air" talent has led her to a partnership working on the development of instructional videos for homeowners.

Retirement from one position is often a time to think about your calling. Guy was an executive director with a nonprofit and used his retirement as a time to look at his values and skills and possible translations for that. At the same time, Guy designed what he wanted to be sure and have in his life and proportionately what percent of his life each thing should be. That allowed him to transition from a life that had a large amount of time devoted to work to a plan to include time for what calls to him and is important to him.

Reinvention occurs at different times in people's lives. It might be a new mom that has decided to change professions so her career gives her more flexibility and time with family, a baby boomer who's retiring but still wants to engage in fulfilling work, a college graduate who's seeking a field that's outside their degree, or someone looking for work that feels like a calling rather than a job. No matter what the circumstances, there are certain steps that hold true for everyone. You'll find as you go through your reinvention process that it's not a linear process. One client, Nadia, made her reinvention plan to pursue a writing career after she'd been directing films. Upon further reflection and exploration, she realized what she really wanted to do was incorporate the writing into the filmmaking. She then revisited some of steps in the reinvention process to include both her passion for writing and filmmaking.

10 STEPS TO YOUR REINVENTION

Here are the steps that will help you on your way to reinvention.

1. Plan ahead. It's important to start thinking about your reinvention early. As you go through the process of figuring out what your reinvention is going to be, you might come up with something that will take time to put in place. Implementing your reinvention might involve taking courses, receiving certification, mentoring with someone, finding a storefront or putting many business operations in place. You need the time to get ready for whatever it is you come up with. The more time you put into planning, the richer it will be.

2. **Reflect on your skills, talents and interests.** The best reinvention is one that's a good match with your skills, talents and interests. Think about how these three areas are currently part of your life, or that might have been a part of your life in the past. What are some potential paths you might consider based on your skills, talents and interests.

3. **Reflect on your passions, values and causes.** Think about possible ways passions, values, and causes could fit into your reinvention. Is there a cause that means a lot to you? Could this cause be a part of your reinvention? You want alignment with these areas and the new path you are designing.

4. **Consider lots of possibilities.** Explore lots of different possibilities while you're reflecting. The more possibilities you consider, the better match you'll be able to come up with for who you uniquely are. Make sure that the possibilities are true to your vision. The clearer your vision is, the easier it will be to expand your possibilities.

5. **Think about geography and work environment.** What area you would like to live in for your reinvention. Is it the same as now, or do you want to live someplace else for your reinvention? Think about where you are at your best. Also consider your work environment. Do you want to be in an office setting, work from home, have your own business location?

6. **Calculate your financial needs.** You need to have a complete picture of your financial obligations at the time of your reinvention and the resources you have to meet them. You should consider any costs that will be involved in preparing for your reinvention and have a realistic idea of the projected income from your reinvention.

7. **Surround yourself with support.** It's helpful to have people around you who believe in what you're doing and can support you on the journey. This can take many different forms: It might be a friend who cheers you on, family members who support you making a change, or a mentor in the field you're interested in pursuing.

8. **Create an advisory board.** Your advisory board can be informal, but they need to know your ideas, plans and best thinking at the moment. Use them to bounce ideas and to serve as a source of knowledge, motivation and encouragement. Think about rounding out the group so that different arenas are represented. Some potential members include someone with a business background, someone who's good at networking and branding, and someone with background or ties to the field you're considering entering. There are lots of different ways you can work with this group. You could ask each person if they would be willing have short conversations with you as things come up, or you could schedule a short conference call once a month and set an agenda that includes updates, thoughts and questions. As you invite people to be a part of the group, you need to define the role you're asking each person to play.

9. **Make a plan.** Figure out what steps you need to take to move in the direction of your calling, what gaps you need to fill, and what you need to put in place. Create a blueprint for your plan, with every step being clearly designed and specific. Include a target date for completion of each step. Find someone to hold you accountable for the timeline connected to each step. You might choose a friend, a peer, or perhaps a professional coach.

10. **Give it a try.** Once you've figured out what your true calling is, have crunched the numbers, and researched what you're thinking about doing, and made your plan, it's time to give it a try. You might try it in a small way at first. It's is a bit like trying something on to see if it fits, dipping your toe in the water, or trying a new food…we give all kinds of new things in our life a try. Your reinvention works the same way. A little test or a first step will let you know what the next step is. The way you could give your new career a try could take many different forms.

Some examples are shadowing someone, volunteering for a job that's in the field you want to enter, an internship or part-time work in your new field.

Finding your calling gives you the greatest net possible in your life. It's a way to move from a job that seems like work into a career that offers fulfillment and joy that's part of your true destiny. You'll be living a life designed by you for you.

About Donna

Donna Rippley is an accredited coach who assists individuals searching for a fulfilling career in line with their gifts and passions. She's a member of International Coach Federation (ICF), the coaching industry's top professional organization. Donna has been seen on NBC, CBS, ABC and Fox affiliates around the country.

Donna holds a master's degree in Education and has a 20-year background in education and public school administration. She has taught at the university level at several institutions. Throughout her career in education, Donna conducted numerous leadership development training sessions for public school administrators. As she became more and more passionate about helping people define and reach their goals, Donna discovered and began to learn about the world of coaching, leading ultimately to her own career transition.

Donna is the owner/president of Best Next U. She has received training in executive and business coaching and has coached other coaches in several countries. Donna conducts both one-on-one and small group coaching sessions as well as speaking engagements. She also organizes and leads reinvention retreats. She's the author of *Reinvention From the Heart,* a forthcoming book featuring the stories of individuals whose career transitions have transformed their lives. The book has an accompanying guide designed to help people discover their "best fit" career transition.

CHAPTER 11

Your Digital DNA: The Building Blocks of Your Online Success

By Lindsay Dicks, Nick Nanton,
JW Dicks & Greg Rollett

"The universe is made of stories, not atoms."—Muriel Rukeyser

Back in the Stone Age—aka, before the internet—your professional reputation was squarely in the hands of the people you associated with. As long as you were honest, reliable and straightforward in your business dealings, that reputation stayed spotless. And whatever you did behind closed doors rarely, if ever, spilled out into your professional world.

Fast forward to today, where, thanks to posts on social media sites and elsewhere on the internet, you're suddenly stuck explaining things you don't want to have to explain to the people you do business with. Those things may seem relatively harmless, but those pictures of you on vacation after a few drinks will suddenly become part of the professional conversation about you.

Your reputation is now at the mercy of Google, Bing and other internet search engines. Think about it: The first thing most of us do when we hear about someone we're interested in doing business with is do a search on their name to see what we can find out. What we find out in that first page of results is critical to how we will view them professionally.

That's why we've spent a lot of time—and an awful lot of money—to unlock the secrets behind all of our "Digital DNA." What we found out can boost your profile, lift your business to the next level, and make you an online superstar.

How? Read on.

BUILDING CELEBRITY EXPERTS

Our agency specializes in building Celebrity Expert® status for our clients. While they're experts in their field, they don't know how to position themselves in their market with the right media for their particular message.

Just like a great movie or book needs the proper publicity launch to make the public aware of their existence, our clients need a certain kind of exposure to communicate their unique personalities, skill sets and experiences to a broader circle of other influential thought leaders and potential customers. We work at making the right connections for them at the right time, using such platforms as bestselling books, programs on network TV affiliates, and articles in national periodicals such as the *Wall Street Journal, Newsweek* and *USA Today.*

Naturally, we promote these media placements through our clients' websites and social media services, such as Facebook, Twitter and so forth, to further boost their brands. This ensures that these prestigious appearances show up as an integral part of their online identity. Note, however, that we said *"part"* of that identity.

The fact is there are a lot of facets to anyone's online identity that we *don't* control in this process. There may still be a lot of other personal or even professional information that might show up that could easily conflict with the main messaging we are putting out about them.

For all the information about yourself that either you or other people leave behind online, we've developed the term, "Digital DNA™." Unlike genetic DNA, this "strand" is one you actually can alter to your benefit. And it can definitely be in your best interests to do so.

GOING DEEPER INTO YOUR DIGITAL DNA™

As we said, your Digital DNA™ is comprised of every byte of information that exists about you in the online world. We're talking about your personal websites and blog posts, Facebook, LinkedIn, YouTube, personal photos, press about you and any other internet site where you've been mentioned or where you've posted something.

If you're like most people, you've probably Googled your name at some point and either been either surprised at the information that's appeared about you—or disappointed that you haven't left more of an online mark. The good news is that both situations can be corrected and should be. Understanding and controlling how you're represented on the internet is the single most important business strategy you should undertake today because again, that's where everyone at this moment in time goes to find out who you are, what you do, and whether you're the person they want to do business with. It's almost like the ultimate job interview—and one that you're not even in the room for!

It's easy to see that your Digital DNA™ contains the building blocks of your success, but it only works that way if it is properly managed and continually updated. If it isn't, your online reputation will remain a big question mark, controlled by unknown factors or, even worse, actually tarnished by other parties you may not even know.

Your offline activities now pale beside your online reputation, which is more easily accessible than ever, because most of us have the internet at our fingertips 24/7. When people want to know about you, they'll instantly jump on their laptop, iPad or smartphone and find out what they can. Even if someone offline personally vouches for you, the internet has become our de facto authority and can trump that recommendation.

That's because, while our memories can fade and grow fuzzy, online info remains as clear as it was the day it was posted, which might have been two, 10 or even 15 years ago. Whatever was said about you in the past, good or bad, right or wrong, isn't going away any day soon.

Because information about you told by anyone right or wrong is so readily available to anyone checking you out, you *must* be constantly aware of your Digital DNA™—and be proactive in controlling what story is being projected online to prospects and customers. This is a quantum shift in how people find out about you and check you out, and many people still haven't caught on to its importance. To ignore the reality of this shift and its consequences, however, is to unnecessarily put your business and reputation at risk.

OUTCLASSING THE COMPETITION

Even if you're confident there's nothing out there online that can really hurt you, there's also an awesome opportunity to use your Digital DNA™, if you're willing to be proactive about it. Controlling your online reputation in order to present yourself in the best possible light to all who search for you means you'll be taking advantage of the incredible untapped potential that the internet offers you to boost your expert status.

As we said, when people perform an online search on your name, it's like the ultimate job interview. Now, imagine going to a job interview in a t-shirt and shorts, instead of your best clothes, that would be more than a little bit crazy, right? Well, not attending to your Digital DNA™ isn't that far from that outlandish example. In every other business situation, you want to look your best, and this vital one is no different?

Odds are, your competition is already hard at work making sure they look *their* best online. Just as you wouldn't be the only applicant participating in a job interview process, you most certainly have other people selling what you're selling online. Your goal should be to "look" better than they do, so you have the leadership position in your field all to yourself. Whoever takes that position as the primary online expert has an obvious and undeniable advantage—and forces everyone else to play catch-up.

When you work your Digital DNA™ to the max, you put yourself in that leadership position.

CLEANING UP YOUR DIGITAL DNA™

The first move you should make to really take control of your DNA is to clean up and cement your current online identity as much as you can. There are four important steps you can take to make that happen.

1. Manage Your Brand

As you set out to tweak your online presences, first *write out who you want to be seen as* when people Google you. Keep that paper with you—and keep that personal image in mind as you participate in online activities of all kinds. Build toward that digital brand. Think of it as a goal and take small steps every day to make it a reality. A great idea is to set aside a half-hour to an hour a day just to focus on your online identity. This can be done by writing blogs and doing press release on the blog you wrote. When you syndicate the press release it will be picked up by online media services, and many will then be posted by the search engines and either the press release, blog or both will appear in a Google search about you. If you do this daily, you'll be adding 365 more items to you Digital DNA™, which will help drive conflicting information about you lower on the search page.

2. Create Consistency

You must make your personal page on Facebook (if you have one) as professional as possible, and make sure all your social media pages reflect the same "you." It's great to showcase family, pets and all other personal activities that show you in a positive light—you just have to make sure nothing shows up that would *conflict with or contradict the online image you want to put out there*. When you post a picture online with you in it, ask yourself the whether you want a future employer to see this picture because there's a good chance they will.

3. Own Your Name

You might be thinking it's more trouble than it's worth to participate in Twitter, Facebook and the like. The advantage, though, of doing that is that the more places you put your name, the more SEO power your Digital DNA™ acquires. Sometimes just a couple of "tweets" can put your name on the first page of Google results—just remember to write about things you want to be associated with!

4. Be Yourself

This might seem to contradict everything we've just discussed, but as the old marketing motto goes, "People buy people." Working with your personality, instead of against it, brings more authentic results than trying to be something you're not. Obviously, you want to put some filters in place and not recount some horrific fight you might have had with your spouse the other night, but you can still use appropriate humor as well as share your hobbies so people can see you're a well-rounded and interesting person.

The key to all of this is follow-through. When you stay on this effort day-in and day-out, it continues to pay off and keeps your name at the top of the online heap.

GOING TO THE NEXT LEVEL

Yes, there's a lot you can do on your own to fine-tune your Digital DNA™ but, at some point, if you're going to want to really make your online reputation pop out in a meaningful and awesome way, getting some expert help is really the best solution.

That's because, to really get proactive with your Digital DNA™ takes a lot of effort and time, as well as some specific skill sets that you may not have. For example, you'll want to distribute online press releases and syndicate them to high-impact sites to really trumpet your business accomplishments and media appearances. You'll also want to consider posting videos based around your area of expertise, as well as creating original content in the form of articles, blogs, webinars, and e-books. This kind of content is important to have posted at different places other than your own personal website. That way, when your name is Googled, you'll look incredibly influential all across the internet.

And speaking of your own website, you'll also want to make sure your website avails itself of the latest SEO techniques, so that it (and you) ranks as high as possible in search engine results.

Putting all these kinds of things in motion really helps you sparkle online. When you create and continue to update a comprehensive and compelling social media presence, as well as generate the content we just described, the more positive "buzz" builds around your name. You decrease the digital "noise" while turning up the volume (and increasing the focus) on your credentials and accomplishments.

That's important, because the more positive content that's connected to you, the higher you rank in online search engines. That directly affects your bottom line in a way you often don't even see, because it's hard to know how much business you're losing, simply because your online "story" isn't coming across correctly. All you can know is that the result is a negative ROI.

There's one thing that science has proved over the years: small changes can have profound effects. Every step you take to promote yourself online in an authentic and impactful way will increase the chance that a prospect will quickly understand the unique features and benefits you alone can provide. At the same time, each informative link you provide back to your talents and services is a new pathway to greater respect and increased revenue.

Whether you know it or not, your Digital DNA™ is already out there—and is directly responsible for whether a potential customer will buy from you or not. If you don't take control of it, it can't work to its fullest extent for you. Even worse, it might even be working against you. By taking action, you have the ability to create an overwhelmingly positive perception that positions you as the celebrity expert in your field. That ultimately results in more sales and increased profits—and isn't that really the best inheritance you can get from your DNA?

About Lindsay

Lindsay Dicks helps her clients tell their stories in the online world. Being brought up around a family of marketers, but a product of Generation Y, Lindsay naturally gravitated to the new world of on-line marketing. Lindsay began freelance writing in 2000 and soon after launched her own PR firm that thrived by offering an in-your-face "Guaranteed PR" that was one of the first of its type in the nation.

Lindsay's new media career is centered on her philosophy that "people buy people." Her goal is to help her clients build a relationship with their prospects and customers. Once that relationship is built and they learn to trust them as the expert in their field, then they will do business with them. Lindsay also built a patent-pending process that utilizes social media marketing, content marketing and search engine optimization to create online "buzz" for her clients that helps them to convey their business and personal story. Lindsay's clientele span the entire business map and range from doctors and small business owners to Inc 500 CEOs.

Lindsay is a graduate of the University of Florida. She is the CEO of CelebritySites™, an online marketing company specializing in social media and online personal brand-ing. Lindsay is also a multi-best-selling author including the best-selling book *Power Principles for Success,* which she co-authored with Brian Tracy. She was also se-lected as one of America's PremierExperts™ and has been quoted in *Newsweek*, the *Wall Street Journal, USA Today,* and *Inc.* magazine as well as featured on NBC, ABC, and CBS television affiliates speaking on social media, search engine optimization and making more money online. Lindsay was also recently brought on FOX 35 News as their Online Marketing Expert.

Lindsay, a national speaker, has shared the stage with some of the top speakers in the world, such as Brian Tracy, Lee Milteer, Ron LeGrand, Arielle Ford, David Bullock, Brian Horn, Peter Shankman and many others. Lindsay was also a Producer on the Emmy-nominated film Jacob's Turn.

You can connect with Lindsay at:
Lindsay@CelebritySites.com
www.twitter.com/LindsayMDicks
www.facebook.com/LindsayDicks

About Nick

An Emmy Award-Winning Director and Producer, Nick Nanton, Esq., is known as the Top Agent to Celebrity Experts around the world for his role in developing and marketing business and professional experts, through personal branding, media, marketing and PR to help them gain credibility and recognition for their accomplishments. Nick is recognized as the nation's leading expert on personal branding as *Fast Company* magazine's Expert Blogger on the subject and lectures regularly on the topic at at major universities around the world. His book *Celebrity Branding You®* has also been used as the textbook on personal branding for University students.

The CEO of The Dicks + Nanton Celebrity Branding Agency, an international agency with more than 1,000 clients in 26 countries, Nick is an award-winning director, producer and songwriter who has worked on everything from large scale events to television shows with the likes of Bill Cosby, President George H.W. Bush, Brian Tracy, Michael Gerber and many more.

Nick is recognized as one of the top thought-leaders in the business world and has co-authored 16 best-selling books alongside Brian Tracy, Jack Canfield (creator of the *Chicken Soup for the Soul* Series), Dan Kennedy, Robert Allen, Dr. Ivan Misner (Founder of BNI), Jay Conrad Levinson (Author of the *Guerilla Marketing* Series), Leigh Steinberg and many others, including the breakthrough hit *Celebrity Branding You!.®*

Nick has published books by Brian Tracy, Mari Smith, Jack Canfield, Dan Kennedy and many other celebrity experts, and Nick has led the marketing and PR campaigns that have driven more than 600 authors to Best-Seller status. Nick has been seen in U*SA Today, Wall Street Journal, Newsweek, Inc.* magazine, *The New York Times, Entrepreneur®* magazine, and FastCompany.com, and has appeared on ABC, NBC, CBS, and FOX television affiliates around the country, as well as CNN, FOX News, CNBC, and MSNBC from coast to coast, speaking on subjects ranging from branding, marketing and law to American Idol.

Nick is a member of the Florida Bar, holds a JD from the University of Florida Levin College of Law, as well as a BSBA in Finance from the University of Florida's Warrington College of Business. Nick is a voting member of The National Academy of Recording Arts & Sciences (NARAS, Home to The GRAMMYs), a member of The National Academy of Television Arts & Sciences (Home to the Emmy Awards), co-founder of the National Academy of Best-Selling Authors, an 11-time Telly Award winner, and spends his spare time working with Young Life and Downtown Credo Orlando and rooting for the Florida Gators with his wife, Kristina, and their three children, Brock, Bowen and Addison.

About JW

JW Dicks, Esq., is America's foremost authority on using personal branding for business development. He has created some of the most successful brand and marketing campaigns for business and professional clients to make them the Credible Celebrity Expert in their field and build multi-million-dollar businesses using their recognized status.

JW Dicks has started, bought, built, and sold a large number of businesses over his 39-year career and developed a loyal international following as a business attorney, author, speaker, consultant, and business expert's coach. He not only practices what he preaches by using his strategies to build his own businesses, he also applies those same concepts to help clients grow their business or professional practice the way he does.

 JW has been extensively quoted in such national media as *USA Today, Wall Street Journal, Newsweek, Inc.* magazine, Forbes.com, CNBC.Com, and Fortune *Small Business*. His television appearances include ABC, NBC, CBS and FOX affiliate stations around the country. He is the resident branding expert for Fast Company's internationally syndicated blog and is the publisher of Celebrity Expert Insider, a monthly newsletter targeting business- and brand-building strategies.

JW has written over 22 books, including numerous best-sellers, and has been inducted into the National Academy of Best Selling Authors. JW is married to Linda, his wife of 39 years, and they have two daughters, two granddaughters and two Yorkies. JW is a 6th generation Floridian and splits time between his home in Orlando and his beach house on the Florida west coast.

About Greg

Greg Rollett, the ProductPro, is a best-selling author and online marketing expert who works with authors, experts, entertainers, entrepreneurs and business owners all over the world to help them share their knowledge and change the lives and businesses of others. After creating a successful string of his own educational products, Greg began helping others in the production and marketing of their own products.

Greg is a front-runner in utilizing the power of social media, direct response marketing and customer education to drive new leads and convert those leads into long-standing customers and advocates.

Previous clients include Coca-Cola, Miller Lite, Warner Bros and Cash Money Records, as well as hundreds of entrepreneurs and small-business owners. Greg's work has been featured on FOX News, ABC, and the Daily Buzz. Greg has written for Mashable, the Huffington Post, AOL, AMEX's Open Forum and more.

Greg loves to challenge the current business environments that constrain people to working 12-hour days during the best portions of their lives. By teaching them to leverage technology and the power of information, Greg loves helping others create freedom businesses that allow them to generate income, make the world a better place and live a radically ambitious lifestyle in the process.

A former touring musician, Greg is highly sought after as a speaker, having appeared on stages with former Florida Gov. Charlie Crist, best-selling authors Chris Brogan and Nick Nanton, as well as at events such as Affiliate Summit.

If you would like to learn more about Greg and how he can help your business, please contact him directly at greg@productprosystems.com or by calling his office at (877) 897-4611.

You can also download a free report on how to create your own educational products at www.productprosystems.com.

CHAPTER 12

7 Steps to Mastering Social Media Marketing

By Hersh Sandhoo

Social media offers a low-cost way to promote your business and engage your customers. You can use social media for a plethora of purposes, including lead generation and customer acquisition, customer retention and support, complaint management, contests and special offers, event promotion, referral marketing, launching new products or services, and increasing brand awareness.

Making sense of all the social media networks can be daunting for any business owner. With so many networks and options it can be difficult to develop an effective social media marketing strategy. While more than 91 percent of companies use some kind of social media, very few have an effective strategy. It's important to identify which social media networks to use and what type of content you want to provide on each network.

The five major social media networks to focus on are Facebook, Twitter, YouTube, Google+, and LinkedIn. While there are other smaller networks that might be worth exploring—if they fit your business model—you'll get your biggest return on investment if you concentrate on the top five.

The seven steps to mastering social media marketing are:

1. Secure your brand

2. Facebook

3. Blogging

4. YouTube

5. Twitter

6. Google+

7. LinkedIn

SECURE YOUR BRAND

While you don't need to create a strategy for each social network right away, you should create your company profiles and secure your brand name to prevent someone else from cybersquatting or trying to dilute your brand. Don't wait until it's too late because most social networks won't release a vanity username unless it's through a court order, even if you own the trademark. When registering your company on the social networks, it's worth taking a minute to add a quick bio and link to your company website to help boost your search engine rankings. You should also add Google+, Facebook "Like," and Twitter widgets to your website.

FACEBOOK

In formulating your overall social media strategy, start with Facebook first. Why? Facebook has the largest number of active users (more than 800 million), great advertiser tools, website widgets and fan pages that are the most business friendly. In fact, with Facebook, you can launch or promote your business with a low marketing budget even if you don't have a website yet.

For example, my wife has always had a passion for fashion and designing her own dresses. To help her launch her part-time business, we simply followed the same 10-step Facebook marketing strategy I use for my clients at Webmation:

1. Create the Facebook fan page.

2. Update the profile information.

3. Post initial content and photos.

4. Recommend to friends, family and existing customers to get 25 fans.

5. Secure a vanity URL.

6. Create a reveal tab.

7. Add Custom Tabs and micro sites to your fan page.

8. Create a contest and integrate your email opt-in form directly into Facebook.

9. Launch a Facebook ad campaign to get more users to the fan page.

10. Post relevant content, promote company events and follow best practices.

In her case, we created her brand Jaja Couture, told people to email her for an order in the "About" section, posted photos of her dresses in organized albums, sent an email to her friends and family, used the share and recommend features in Facebook, secured the vanity URL facebook.com/jajacouture, and created a simple "like our fan page" contest to win a chance at a free custom-made dress.

We spent just $500 on a Facebook ad campaign. The great thing about Facebook is that the demographic data and audience size is unparalleled. Whereas in Google AdWords, you're showing your ads to people who are actively searching for specific keywords, Facebook allows you to contact your ideal audience even if they're not searching for your product or service.

We identified her ideal target audience: Asian Indian women between the ages of 25 and 40 who live in the United States. While Facebook does not allow you to search by ethnicity, we were still able to tap into the Asian Indian market by selecting keywords that are related to them, such as Bollywood, sarees, Punjabi and Hindi. We then restricted the ad display geographically to the United States and to women who are between the ages of 25 and 40, which are standard options in Facebook Ads.

We structured the ad so the user could like the fan page by clicking the "Like" button directly on the ad. The benefit of doing it this way is that the user can see the names of their friends who already like the page and the total amount of "likes" directly in the ad without leaving the page they're currently on or stopping the game they're playing. Additionally, people who fit the targeted demographic and who have friends that already like the ad would more likely be shown the ad than a random person, creating a viral effect.

If a user clicked the ad, they were directed to a custom tab page that described the contest and had graphics pointing for the person to like the page to enter to win. We also put samples of her work and testimonials on the page, with an email opt-in box for them to sign up for special offers and news.

In less than two weeks we were able to gain over 2,500 highly targeted fans. Then throughout the year, we continued to post photos of new dresses and encouraged buyers to send in their photos wearing their Jaja Couture dresses. We then posted them and tagged the person in it. This is an important step as it allows the user's friends to interact with the photo and be exposed to your brand. One note of caution, don't spam people by tagging them if they're not in the photo. This will just damage your brand's reputation. We also started auto-posting her Facebook updates to Twitter.

We promoted her Open House event exclusively through Facebook and streamed it live directly on her fan page by embedding a live web stream in a custom reveal tab. A reveal tab is a custom tab on your fan page that forces a user to like your brand before they can access the content. This way, only fans or people who liked her page could view the show. The users who were not fans saw a page showing what time the broadcast was to start and instructing them to like the page so they could view the fashion show live.

The results after a year with only putting in a few hours a week into the business were very good. Her fan page grew to over 5,200 targeted fans purely through viral likes, shares and tagged photos. We didn't do any other Facebook advertising after the initial $500 amount. More important, she received custom design orders worth more than $45,000 in sales.

Any company can follow this same 10-step Facebook marketing strategy and grow even faster by increasing their Facebook advertising spend, advertising consistently, having more contests and engaging their audience more. The more interactive you make your page, the more fans will stick around and recommend your page.

Example: http://facebook.com/webmation

BLOGGING

When blogging, you're posting articles, stories, news, events, contests, special offers, photos and thoughts about current topics to position yourself as an expert in your industry. Users can comment and engage you on your blog, and you can post your content in a more organized manner than on the social networks. Your blog is all about you, so you're not competing with other companies while a visitor is reading your articles.

Install a WordPress blog on your own domain name and include the Facebook, Google+ and Twitter plug-ins to allow users to share your content on those networks. Setup a Digg, Reddit and StumbleUpon account and also include the share plug-ins for them on your articles. These are the most popular sharing sites for news and blog content. I also recommend using Disqus for handling comments as it allows users to login from various email and social media accounts.

When updating your statuses on other social networks link back to your blog articles. This will also allow users to easily share your articles with their friends. It's also a good idea to code your blog links as HTML pages instead of using the category ID format for better search engine indexing.

Example: http://www.becominglegendary.com

YOUTUBE

After establishing your Facebook and blog presence, move on to YouTube. YouTube is the largest video-based social network boasting more than 158 million visits per month. Your goal is to gain subscribers and drive traffic from YouTube back to your website, blog or Facebook fan page by posting relevant and unique videos to their site. YouTube videos also play well when linked inside of Facebook and Google+.

Make sure to build out your profile and put links back to your site in the video descriptions. How-to and instructional videos, humorous commentaries, behind the scenes, sneak peak previews, product demonstrations and customer testimonials are great videos to post. One mistake some small businesses make is thinking the videos have to be polished productions. On the contrary, viral home-grown videos do very well.

Example: http://youtube.com/thewpsn

TWITTER

Twitter is a unique social media network that allows its 100 million active users to post status updates and multimedia links that are limited to just 140 characters. New customer acquisition on Twitter can be difficult unless you're a celebrity or established brand. By growing your customer base and promoting your Twitter account on your site and blog you'll drive more people to become followers.

You should begin to differentiate the content you place on the networks. This encourages your customers to follow you on multiple platforms. For example, many companies use Twitter for customer support and sending important updates to clients. You should also encourage conversations about your brand, events and promotions using hashtags (#topic).

As you funnel more Facebook fans and customers into becoming Twitter followers, you can have contests that ask followers to retweet your update for a chance to win the prize. Avoid following random people just to increase your fan base because it won't do much to help your business and even with software takes quite a bit of management. However, you can search for people who are tweeting about your brand or industry and engage them.

Example: http://twitter.com/webmation

GOOGLE+

Google+ is Google's answer to Facebook. The possibilities for integration with Google's search, YouTube and Google +1 button may have a larger impact in the future when it comes to your Google search rankings. Since Google has such a larger user base with its other services, its 90 million Google+ user base will continue to grow.

The main drawback of Google+ for business is that it doesn't allow contests or promotions. Company pages also don't have the ability to have a vanity URL unless using a third-party service like gplus.to.

However, posting on Google+ may allow you to tap into a different audience of more tech-savvy early adopters. The strategy for posting videos, photos and status updates is the same with Facebook.

Example: http://gplus.to/webmation

LINKEDIN

LinkedIn is a professional social media network. It allows companies, executives and other professionals to communicate, seek employment or employees, get endorsements, and meet new people through recommendations and groups. User profiles read like resumes and are linked to their company profiles on the site. LinkedIn can also be used for business to business sales, customer acquisition, and help with your website's search engine rankings. The average LinkedIn user has an income of more $100,000 a year in the United States. Like the other social media networks, you can post status updates, links, photos and videos. LinkedIn also allows you to integrate your blog and Twitter feed into the site for more visibility.

Example: http://www.linkedin.com/in/webmation

KEEP INFORMED

While social media marketing is an extremely powerful business tool, it also has the potential for disaster. There are many horror stories of companies and people making silly mistakes that cost them reputation, customers or their jobs.

It's important to keep your finger on the pulse of the latest trends and best practices. To gain free access to Webmation's client-only social media best practices guide, join our newsletter, and to see successful social media case studies, visit www.webmation.com/nothingbutnet.

About Hersh

Hersh Sandhoo has been labeled a marketing and programming genius by industry leaders. He has generated more than $100 million in leads, sales, referrals and cost savings for his clients over the past decade. Hersh is best known for being able to create niche solutions and systems to automate businesses into revenue-making machines. With ownership in more than eight companies, Hersh uses the same strategies he shares with his clients to expand his own portfolio.

As president and CEO of Webmation, Hersh helps clients create comprehensive marketing and business systems that bridge the gap between offline and online marketing. By providing all the marketing services companies need to be successful, he has eliminated the need for businesses to deal with more than 20 different providers for the same range of services.

Webmation provides complete marketing systems that include web development, HTML email marketing, e-commerce, online and social media marketing, event promotion and merchant services, video production, direct mail, graphic design, QR codes, digital photography, CRM and online training solutions. Webmation also boasts its own in-house print shop and provides clients access to more than 900,000 promotional products.

Webmation has serviced a wide array of companies, including Comcast SportsNet, Maryland State Department of Education, Paramount, Marketing Legend Jay Abraham, American College of Sports Development, and thousands of small to medium businesses worldwide.

Hersh has also been featured on WUSA9 News, WHUR 96.3FM, NBC4 Health Expo, Affiliate Summit West, Martial Arts Millionaire Bootcamp, NAPMA World Conference, Self-Defense Forum, *The Truth About the Martial Arts Business, Martial Arts Professional, Feedfront* magazine, *Gazette* and DirectReponse.Net.

He's the author of the popular blog "Becoming Legendary" and is the author of the upcoming book, *Beast Mode Marketing.* To connect with Hersh online:
- *Blog:* http://becominglegendary.com
- *Twitter:* http://twitter.com/hersh01
- *Facebook:* http://facebook.com/becominglegendary
- *LinkedIn:* http://linkendin.com/in/webmation
- *Google+:* http://gplus.to/hersh01

To learn how Webmation can help you systemize your business and marketing, visit http://www.webmation.com or call (855) WEBMATION.

CHAPTER 13

Stop Selling, Start Listening: How to Transform Ordinary Contacts Into Customers

By Robert Parkerson

It was a dreary, rainy spring day as I opened the envelopes from the mailbox. One of them was the cell phone bill. As I opened the bill, my gut filled with disgust. After considering my contempt, I realized there was no further obligation on my part to my current cell phone company, as my contract had expired. I had gotten sick of the poor customer service and unexplainable charges from my current carrier, so I decided to go out in search of a "new beginning." Since I live in a town with several retail stores (which sell and service all types of phones from different carriers), my journey began to free myself from the bondage of the company whose "customer care" department didn't really care!

I was warmly greeted as I walked through the front door of one of the local wireless carriers near the mall. "May I help you, sir?" a nice young lady said with a smile. An interesting choice of words, to be sure, especially since the next few moments of interaction would prove to me to be the exact opposite of the question which she had posed.

You see, she had been trained to ask this question as new faces walked in the front door, and she had become very proficient in doing so. Unfortunately, this is where her training had stopped and her inexperience in human interaction began to become apparent. I tried to explain my situation to her as she obliviously nodded her head and moved me toward a wall with what seemed like an endless array of phones.

She hadn't heard a word I had said and began immediately to try to sell me the most popular and trendy phone that was available. I wasn't there to be "sold." Most of us never are. I was interested in gaining enough information to make an intelligent and informed decision that I was comfortable with in my life.

The young sales associate tried diligently with her best efforts of wit and charm to get me to understand all about the features and the bells and whistles of the phone that I should, at least in her mind, be so interested in and absolutely overtaken by, that I would run to the counter and beg her to sign me up.

She had lost me. I couldn't keep up with the conversation that she was attempting to have with me. I began to see myself shaking my head as if I were listening, just as she had done with me in the beginning our of time together. You and I both know that by this point that I wasn't really listening and was simply appeasing her to be kind.

After a few moments, I thanked her for her time and dismissed myself from her presence. She very graciously thanked me for coming in and walked away, onto the next customer who was walking in the front door. Boy, was I glad I wasn't in his shoes at that moment!

I immediately walked up to the counter and asked to see the manager. I explained to the manager many of the things that had happened and asked if there was someone else who could help me without duplicating this sequence of events. The manager grabbed one of the other sales ladies on the floor and asked her to assist me and to try and understand what I was interested in. This new sales associate offered me her hand to shake as she greeted me, and within 10 seconds, I *knew* that this would be the person with whom I would be doing business. Let me explain.

Mary (not her real name) began to immediately ask me questions and write down my responses. She was very interested in all the things I had to say and all of the questions I had for her regarding several of my choices in phones. She was patient and kind, and at no time did I feel rushed or pressured to make a decision where she was concerned. She didn't pretend to hear me; she actually wrote down my questions and referred back to them, then asked if my questions had been answered to my satisfaction.

Mary spent 45 minutes or more with me, invoking great curiosity and apparent jealousy on the part of my first sales associate, as she would occasionally glare in our direction and seemingly give an angry look to Mary. Mary never seemed to mind as she continued in her patient demeanor to answer each and every concern I would throw her way.

I had finally narrowed it down to two choices, so we began to compare only the features and benefits of each of the choices before me. Mary kindly followed me from one side of the store to the other as I tried to sort all of the details in my mind from the enormous amount of information I had been given.

Seeing my dilemma, Mary asked for one of the other sales associates to tell me about her experience with the phone I obviously favored. I heard the testimonial and that made it real for me. Mary had skillfully moved my focus from herself to a third party and had someone else who had no "skin in the game" to give a testimonial, which helped me justify my decision.

With a few more really insignificant questions, which were effortlessly answered, I had made up my mind and purchased my new phone. I'm quite certain that Mary received the commission for the sale and has probably long since forgotten about me. However, this experience is one I will not likely soon forget.

Let's go back and look at the situation. If you've ever been in a sales situation, ask yourself whether or not you were the first salesperson, or if you were more like Mary with your customers.

One thing I'm certain of is that no one cares how much you know until they're sure you've heard their concerns. I've been in countless sales scenarios where I wanted to impress my audience with all of the neat things I knew about my industry, my company, my product or service. And impress them, I did. They went home impressed, and I went home broke. I couldn't understand how *anyone* could hear what I had to say and how great my product or service was and *not* buy from me. I mean, I had gone to all the training classes, the seminars, the continuing education, and I was the best of the best in my field. No one knew more about my product than me—I made absolutely certain of it!

The problem was that when I was in front of a potential customer, I had become much like the first sales associate in the previous scenario. I was so impressed with myself and what I was going to be able to do for my prospect, and how I was going to be able to improve their lives, that I forgot to *listen*.

There's an old saying in the sales world: "If your mouth is moving, you are losing." Sales is and always has been about helping the consumer make a more informed and educated decision to benefit from the product or service that you have to offer (and that we hope that they wish to own) but only *after* we listen and hear what the consumer *really* wants. Become a master of listening, understanding and *then* educating, and you'll become a master of a large bank account.

The first step is not only to listen to the prospect and their concerns, but it has to do with *how* you listen. Listening is the second most important part of this entire equation. Second? I'll explain more about what that means later.

People are taught in school to read, write, do mathematics equations and a host of other topics, but I cannot remember taking a class on listening. I do remember taking a speech class, however.

The purpose of true "active" listening must clearly be defined before we can move forward.

It doesn't matter if you're talking about relationships between married couples, family members, prospective clients or customers. The purpose of listening is almost never just to "hear" but to clarify, decipher, discern, reflect, and create a conclusion about what has been heard. Listening is the first step in creating a dialogue (which happens to be Greek for "through words).

It has been said that perhaps the most important factor in listening is to develop, sustain, enhance and anchor a relationship. Whether that relationship is being built as a simple acquaintance, a good friend, a lover, or maybe even transforming a prospect into a lifelong customer; the process is ultimately the same. And whatever your purpose may be, you'll almost certainly be pleased with the results if you gain a deeper understanding of these principles and follow the formula.

In other words, it's not just listening but knowing *why* you are listening and *what* you're listening for. This self-examination causes us to explore the deeper meanings of our conversations and really helps us to clarify the other person's true intentions.

Let's consider our methods of listening at their very core to help us gain a better understanding of exactly where we may have been missing opportunities to be of better service to those with whom we wish to more effectively communicate. Though there are many different types of listening, we ultimately are only concerned with an understanding of *how* to listen properly so that we may better serve our customers and ultimately have them refer more business to us. Right?

To me, the greatest method of demonstrating to the other party that we are truly concerned about whatever it is that they may be speaking about is to ask questions. Dig for more information. Most of the time, people will be happy to give it to you.

Listening is actually the second most important piece of the puzzle. I just gave you the first! *Ask* questions, then *ask* questions and then *ask* some more questions. Asking questions gives the prospect an opportunity to do what they love to do. Remember, people love to talk. And the one thing that they love to talk most about is what? Themselves! Why would we take that away from them? I'll tell you exactly why…because we want to talk about ourselves, too! *Shut up and let them talk!*

Asking questions also positions you as someone who's genuinely caring, and it draws people closer to you. If we don't interrupt and learn how to become sincerely interested in their problems, concerns, and personal or business situations, in most cases we'll gain the prospect's trust and ultimately their business.

More than 80 percent of sales are lost because a typical salesperson pounces as soon as the prospect starts to take a breath. *Stop!* Take a moment and count to five before you respond to anything your prospect says.

Understanding "how" we listen is especially important to those of us in the sales world simply because we need to understand the psyche of the person on the other side of the table and how they're looking at or evaluating the ideas we may be offering them. We all discern and discriminate based on our own knowledge, prejudices, past experiences, and most important, our values. Keep this thought in mind as you are dealing with prospects.

So many people believe that selling is about persuading someone to believe the way we do or buy the product or service that we're selling. We need to remember that if we stop selling and truly start listening to the needs of others and applying the information they've given us, we'll find that they'll become much more agreeable to the product or service we have to offer (so long as it answers a need or desire in their life).

It's my belief that many people don't have more customers because they try too hard to sell, instead of getting to know the person and their needs. I always enjoyed having a product that "sells itself," because it allowed me to shut up. I cannot tell you the number of times I've let people talk until they talk themselves right into buying from me!

This is the first of three steps in understanding the true mastery of the sales process. There are other "keys" that you need to know to make the formula complete, and I'm always happy to get those keys into your hands. Simply contact me directly at www.stopsellingstartlistening.com. Until we meet again; may God bless and keep you, and may you live life to its most enormous potential!

About Robert

Robert Parkerson is a professional speaker, author and success coach who's delivered more than 1,000 presentations in the area of sales, educational training, leadership and motivation.

Robert has more than 20 years of very successful applied business experience in the private and public sectors. He's the founder and CEO of RPI Inc., and with more than 20 years of very successful applied business experience in the public and private sectors is making a difference in the lives of thousands of people all across the United States and Canada with his speaking venues and private coaching and consulting programs.

Robert has owned several very successful businesses and is very results-oriented, but left the field of financial planning after 14 years to pursue his dream of helping others with his passion of public speaking, coaching and training. He has read literally hundreds of books on success and personal development and has recently authored the top-selling book *Stop Selling, Start Listening: The Three Keys to Transforming Ordinary Contacts Into Customers, Referrals and Repeat Business.*

Robert has been in the top 5 percent of sales professionals with every company he has represented and, as a result, has received many awards and honors, including the Chairman's Award for Excellence from Mainstreet Financial Group, the Diamond Leadership Award from the Alabama Society for Entrepreneurs, and the Rising Star Award from World Marketing Alliance, among many others.

Today, he's known as America's leading authority on relationship selling. For more information about booking Robert to teach you how to dramatically increase your production and your bottom line, contact him directly at www.stopsellingstartlistening. com or by phone/email at (256) 467-1089/stopsellingstartlistening@yahoo.com.

CHAPTER 14

6 Steps to an Explosive Marketing Campaign

By Chris Goff

During my last five years of research, I discovered a major shift in the way people responded to traditional marketing tactics. This is due in part to instability in the economy but also because of a flood of fly-by-night investing guru's and their shady protégés throwing up ugly yellow "we buy houses" signs and scamming people.

I'd been using similar signs and wording in my newspaper ads for years but began noticing a slow-down and a more negative charge in the air when contacting new leads. I found myself saying "No, I'm not those people" more and more often, so I decided it was time to find a way to distinguish my business from "those people." I started with a distinctive logo and color scheme for my signs, and carried it over to business cards, postcards, website and the like. But I didn't stop with branding. I experimented with different types of wording in my ads and websites, and soon I began to see an overwhelming response from buyers and sellers. I implemented these changes in my students' businesses, and they received the same phenomenal results.

What I learned was that, just like in every other market today, the real estate consumer is more conservative. They research more before buying, and they respond better to a more professional marketing approach.

In this chapter, we'll cover six basic steps that any business can use to improve its marketing. The fundamentals are the same, no matter what type of product or service you're offering, and the platforms are the same as well. It's knowing what to say and how to say it that makes all the difference in the world!

GETTING STARTED

If you have a product or service that helps people, then you should be making a lot of money. That's because right now—at this very moment—someone is on the internet, reading a newspaper, checking their mailbox, searching for your service or product.

Problem is...they can't find you. But if you know how to get your product or service in front of them, not only will you be able to solve their problem, but you'll also be able to make a lot of money. In fact, marketing your product or service is actually pretty simple...as long as you understand the formula.

Once you do, all that's left to do is cash the checks.

The most important thing to remember during *every* step of your marketing process is that *buyers buy on emotion*. This isn't a new idea. It's been around since the first product was sold thousands of years ago. But it's the easiest thing to forget when putting together a marketing campaign. In the steps below, notice how this idea plays an important role in every step of my Explosive Marketing Formula.

MARKETING STEP 1:
IDENTIFY YOUR PRODUCT OR SERVICE

No matter if you sell a product, service or both, you'll need to learn how to market it. You should work with the way you word your product or service; give it a catchy, unique name. People want to see something new! Give your product some flair by labeling it differently than everyone else.

What's In a Name?

You've heard the saying "A rose by any other name would smell as sweet." This is true, but how many would flower vendors sell on Valentines Day if they were called Thornweed? And would fast-food drive-thrus be as successful if they named their creations "Blubber-burgers and grease fries"? The world is full of alternative names for products and services to make them more appealing to the consumer. Remember, buyers buy on emotion more than anything else. And the emotions that sell are as varied as the products being sold. In general, though, consumers want to buy things that make them feel:

1. *Smarter:*
   - Wise Choice Car Wash
   - Smart Car
   - Petsmart

2. *Special, like they're buying the best:*
   - Royal Lawn Services
   - Regal Painters
   - BestBuy

3. *Convenient:*
   - Express Cleaners
   - QuickLube
   - RoadRunner
   - Easy-Mart

4. *Unique, One-of-a-Kind:*
   - Pier One Imports
   - Custom Choppers
   - Just For Men

New Vs. Established

Consumers get excited over something new and hip just as often as with something established and trustworthy. This doesn't necessarily need to be reflected in the name itself; a tagline below it can work just as well. Decide what message you want to convey and what emotion you want to evoke with your marketing.

Here are some examples:

- New Era Realtors
- "Providing a fresh approach to listing your home!"
- Kenmore Appliances, "A name you can trust!"

The easiest way to evoke emotion goes back to your days in middle school grammar. Know your adjectives, and don't be afraid to use them! Here are some great adjectives to use: innovative, essential, exceptional, comfortable, delicious, trustworthy, royal, safe, intelligent, fast, traditional, value, luxury, easy, friendly, smart

You get the picture!

MARKETING STEP 2: BENEFITS

One of the most important parts of the formula is *benefits*. Benefits show the consumer how your product or service will enhance their lives if they purchase it. Emotions feed off benefits, and it's one of the key factors why people buy. Yet most businesses don't understand exactly what a benefit really is.

For example, "great location" is often used as a benefit when marketing real estate. But this is really a vague, bland sort of term, and doesn't have a very strong effect on the buyers' emotions. A better phrase would be "enjoy shorter commutes and more time spent with family."

This is a real benefit that the buyer can *feel*.

MARKETING STEP 3: PAIN OF NOT BUYING YOUR PRODUCT OR SERVICE

Another important part of your marketing is mentioning the *pain* of not buying your product or service. This part is extremely easy to do because the "pains" are the opposite of the "benefits." We use the pain of not buying your product or service to show the consumer what may happen if they don't purchase.

For continuity, we'll stick with the location theme:

"Tired of long, irritating commutes? Don't miss out on another soccer game because you're stuck in traffic."

Pains remind the consumer of why they're seeking out your product/ service in the first place.

MARKETING STEP 4: PILE ON THE FEATURES OF YOUR PRODUCT OR SERVICE

Many people don't understand the difference between features and benefits, and unfortunately, this can be a huge detriment when you're writing product copy. If you're not describing the right aspects or characteristics of your product or service, then you could be wasting your time by trying to sell something that your target audience doesn't want or need. What's the difference between a feature and a benefit?

A *feature* is a physical or tangible aspect of, or a factual statement about, a product or service you're promoting.

A *benefit* is what happens to your customers when they take your product or service and implement it. In other words, a benefit tells your customers *why* your features matter or "what's in it for them."

While product features are usually easy to detect and describe, product benefits can be trickier because they're often intangible. The most compelling product benefits are those that provide emotional or financial rewards. It's not the brighter smile the toothpaste offers that is it's benefit; it's what the smile might bring you (friends, a better job).

MARKETING STEP 5: THE REASON WHY

There must always be a reason why you're selling anything. It sounds crazy because people don't ask why you're selling a six-piece nugget at McDonald's, but people are curious why you do what you do and sell what you sell. More important, people want to know why they need your product or service.

You must always address both sides of the "why":

1. Why you are selling?

2. Why they need your product or service?

Your reason doesn't have to be drawn out; it can be simple and short. When you're dealing with real estate, a few examples of this would be:

- We have a baby on the way and need to upsize.
- We need to downsize.
- We have a job transfer.
- We're tired of tenants.

You should include several reasons why the buyer needs your product or service throughout your ad. A great tip for this is to list as many benefits of your product or service as you can, and think of reasons why they're benefits. Great examples of this would be:

- You'll save more time and money.
- You'll enjoy the lovely backyard because of the privacy.
- You can relax in your lovely pool without the hindrance of noisy neighbors.
- This location offers the best public school system in the city.

After you state your reasons, you need to support them. A good way to support reasons is to give specific examples. Specific examples can be names of people, places, things or events.

MARKETING STEP 6: CALL TO ACTION

The "Call to Action" is one of the most important concepts in marketing and promotion. Simply put, after you've established that you have something of value to offer and you're the perfect choice to deliver it, you want to ask your prospect to take the next step, so you deliver a call to action.

Your "call to action" should always be at the end of your marketing ad. When using a website to promote your product or service, however, you may want to place "call to action" buttons throughout your page.

Let's look at some examples:

- *Click Here:* The classic and quintessential call-to-action example for the net. Couple this with other motivational copy.
- *I Invite You To...* People usually get caught off-guard by any kind of manners on the internet—a place not known for abundant etiquette.
- *Get a Free...* This one is completely open-ended and pretty straightforward. People love free stuff, and offering free incentives is one of the best ways to motivate your audience to do anything you want.

- *While Supplies Last:* You hear this one on infomercials all the time. This moves people to act while what they want is still around.

- *Offer Expires:* By giving a date in which your offer expires, people have incentive to act today and ASAP.

- *Satisfaction Guaranteed:* People love guarantees. People love satisfaction. Just put them together.

- *Get It Now!* No wait, plenty of immediacy and the exclamation point really gets attention.

- *1 Million Satisfied Customers:* Social proof can be very effective as a call to action. People don't like to take risks of any kind when it comes to the internet or consumerism; seeing that you have lots of other satisfied customers who've come before them and done what they're about to do is important for some people.

- *Free Consultation:* Your doors are open. You're offering free information.

- *Learn the Biggest Mistakes...* Tweak your reader's curiosity whenever possible.

- *Offer Expires at Midnight:* Another time-based call-to-action example. The verb "expire" is certainly strong language as well.

- *Order Now and Receive a Free Gift:* An incentive-based example.

- *3 Days Only/Just 3 More Days:* Similar to other ticking-clock offers, giving a specific timeframe certainly motivates people to take action sooner than later.

An effective call to action, if done right, can generate real measurable return on investment, and in the current economic climate, this is what we all want.

WHERE TO APPLY MARKETING STEPS

Regardless of how you advertise your product or service, you'll need to market it where people are searching for the product or service you're offering. You wouldn't advertise a diet product in a blog that talks about building race cars. You would market the product where people are interested in learning more about weight loss, such as health magazines, fitness clubs, weight-loss blogs and forums. The biggest mistake I see most people make when marketing their business is to place ads in places that don't suit their consumer.

There are many websites you can market your business on for free, such as Craigslist, Backpage and your own website. You should also look into using social media sites to get the word out. Some great free ones include Facebook, Twitter and YouTube. Get started writing blogs to work on building an audience. The power of the blog is infinite when it comes to spreading the word about "the next big thing."

Keep in mind, the only thing that will make your marketing better is practice. Keep moving forward and never become discouraged. You'll soon realize what works and what doesn't.

About Chris

Chris Goff started real estate investing in 1999. He didn't have any money to work with, so he was interested in learning "no money down" strategies. He absorbed any and every bit of information he could find on the subject and started on his first deal. Chris was lucky enough to break even on the deal and quickly learned that not all information is good information.

Chris continued learning from his mistakes and began to see some pretty amazing results. He took what he learned from others and combined it with what he learned by trial and error, to develop a system that would produce as much income as possible, without many of the pitfalls found in real estate investing. In his first 20 months, Chris Goff did 46 deals with no money down. It didn't take long for those around him to figure out that Chris was onto something good, and they began to ask him how he was doing it. Chris explained his system to one person; one led to two, two led to four, four led to 40, and working for Donald Trump, writing books, programs, and teaching materials for his real estate education company. Chris learned a valuable lesson while with Trump. Anyone can *do* real estate, many can *speak* about it, but not everyone can *teach* it. In this, Chris Goff has a genuine gift.

During his time with Trump University, Chris mentored hundreds of budding real estate investors. The impressive level of success that his students were able to achieve, plus the perfect satisfaction ratings that Chris received, led to an invitation to head up Trump's in-field training program. In this position, he trained the other mentors in his unique teaching style and wrote the Apprenticeship Program, Fast Track to Foreclosures, Real Estate Blueprint, In-Field Training Program, and the Quick-Start Program. In two years, Chris helped develop more than 70 real estate investment companies as well.

Chris never stops to rest on his laurels, however. Chris and his team are constantly searching for ways to improve their real estate investing approach and teaching technique, doing what so many people fail to achieve—keeping on top of a constantly fluctuating market. To contact Chris, visit him and the REI&ME team at www.REIANDME.com, or call them at (877) 781-7379!

CHAPTER 15

Lessons Learned From Champions, Leaders and Great Businesses

By Christine Rae

"He who dies with the most toys, wins." Over the years, I've found inspiration in the words of others, learning from successful businesspeople, politicians, thought leaders and more. But I'm starting with that famous quote from billionaire Malcolm Forbes, which I first heard back in the late '80s, because it had the *opposite* effect on me.

To me, the idea of a life lived in pursuit of gathering stuff you can't take with you left me feeling hollow and sad. So I decided that in my life, success would be something different, something fulfilling. I made a conscious decision to be the best I could be but not at the expense of my life, my friends, my family or my health. That was the way I wanted to live my life and live my success.

PLAYING TO WIN

Back when I first entered the business world, there weren't a lot of female business leaders. I suppose that's why the analogies and quotes that really stuck with me from that time come from the world of sports. Like Vince Lombardi's famous line: *"If it doesn't matter who wins or loses, then why do they keep score?"*

I learned about competition at an all-girls high school. We played field hockey, I ran in harrier meets for my city, and, as an adult, I developed quite a good game of tennis. And while I've never been able to stand just sitting and watching sports, I've always enjoyed *playing* the game.

Playing to win—in sports, at cards, in business, even in a relationship—requires discipline, strategy, determination and a no-quit attitude. After all, giving up is easy. But staying in the game and getting back up when you fall isn't just important because it's essential to winning—it's essential because it shapes your character, broadens your experience, and generally makes you into a better person. It teaches you to deal with adversity, which I think is the most important skill you need to ultimately achieve success.

The truth is that learning to fail—learning *from* failure—is essential to success. Or as Napoleon Hill wrote in his timeless classic *Think and Grow Rich*, "Every failure will teach you a lesson you need to learn, if you'll keep your eyes and ears open and be willing to be taught. Every adversity is usually a blessing in disguise. Without reverses and temporary defeat, you would never know the sort of metal of which you are made."

BUILDING A BUSINESS

I grew up in the UK, but as an entrepreneur, I feel a real kinship with North America. North America was built by the entrepreneurial visions of people who wanted to carve out a better life for themselves. Today—centuries later—there are more start-up entrepreneurs than ever before. Blame it on the global economic fiasco that hit in 2008—the lack of jobs forced a lot of people to look for opportunity elsewhere. But as Marianne Williamson said, "We are all meant to shine…greatness is in all of us." Self-employment and entrepreneurship offer an incredible opportunity to do just that.

My journey to entrepreneurship started before the economic crash. For me, it came at the end of the year 2000, when the company I was working for reconstructed...or right-sized...or downsized...or whatever you want to call it. The bottom line was that I was suddenly unemployed. I knew I needed to replace my lost income, but I also looked at my newfound "freedom"—at least from my job—as an opportunity. Finally, I could take control and shape the kind of life I wanted. I could go back to the promise I made myself in the '80s and make breathing space, life, health, friends and family my main priorities, in addition to my career.

But like most people just starting out on my own, I encountered a few bumps in the road. I first tried to qualify for government funding to start a business, but the waiting period to be accepted into their program was too long. So I decided to do it on my own, and by June 2001, I found my feet and launched my business—developing, learning, tweaking, nurturing and morphing my services until I found a road that suited me well. I loved my work, I was happy, and most important, I had achieved the balance I had been looking for between work, life and family.

Of course, in business and in life, nothing stays the same forever. After nearly five years, there was a total shift in my business that led to the creation of the company I have now.

GROWTH AND SUCCESS

Back in September 2005, CSP International™ Business Training Academy was just a seed. It was a three-day program I developed to train people who were interested in launching a business in a new field, called home staging. This involved decorating homes that were listed for sale in hopes of generating more, bigger offers in what was (at the time) an exploding real estate market.

That market may have crashed, but my business only grew: By 2009, I employed a full-time staff of 11 and a growing team of top training facilitators teaching the three-day program across the country. We expanded into a 4,000-square-foot sustainable company headquarters, with satellite offices in Sydney, Australia, and Minneapolis, Minnesota. We added additional support programs and services, generated press, pursued and won awards, created a professional industry and developed certification, continuing education classes and an award-winning industry magazine. More important, we changed the way real estate will be sold forever.

I'm proud that CSP International has served as an incubator, a source of information, and a guide for entrepreneurially-minded individuals who want a faster route to profits and success. It makes me feel good knowing I'm helping in some small way to launch thousands of people—mostly other women—to fulfill their own destiny. Like Winston Churchill said, "What is the use of living, if it be not to strive for noble causes and to make this muddled world a better place for those who will live in it after we are gone?" The best part of my success is knowing that other people have benefitted from what I have created—not just me and my family.

That doesn't mean it's easy. There are definitely times when I question my own sanity. But I just keep going, even when it feels like a challenge might derail me. At times, when I start to question whether or not it's all worth it, I remember the words of the great American architect Frank Lloyd Wright, "The thing *always* happens that you truly believe in; and it is the *belief* in the thing which makes it happen." I tell you, that phrase alone has helped me through more sticky points than anything else!

I also find inspiration in the experiences of others. I think of those brave souls who knew the rest of the world thought they were crazy but went ahead and "did it anyway." It motivates and inspires me to know there are generations of people before me who've settled new worlds, created new products and systems—and, in their own way, changed the world. From the Wright brothers to Thomas Edison, from Boadicea, a famous queen of ancient Briton who led a rebellion against the Roman occupiers, to Emily Pankhurst, a British suffragette who battled for women's rights, I've found inspiration in so many stories.

That doesn't mean I'm comparing myself to any of those amazing people—it's just that they inspire me to think of the millions more who've played smaller roles in making the world better. I know there's no reason why I can't be one of them.

On a visit to the UK about 10 years ago, I was in the old city of York at a site where an ancient Viking village had been unearthed. When I toured the exhibit and the museum, I was astounded by how similar life was then. Yes, there was the obvious exception of modern life being more comfortable, but a thousand years ago people went to work, had families and pets, cooked, loved, laughed and died.

Then what's it all about? Why are we here?

WHAT DOES IT ALL MEAN?

My personal philosophy is that we're all here to do good and do well. Or as Plato said, "The meaning of life is in attaining the highest form of knowledge, which is the Idea (form) of the Good, from which all good and just things derive utility and value. Human beings are duty-bound to pursue the good." If you Google the question, "Why are we here?" you'll find hundreds more philosophers and other people who are much smarter than me who believe the same thing. What you do with your life matters. And yet, too many people live as if we get more than one go-around.

Of course, our own emotions can work against us. When I teach, the one emotion I encounter most often in students setting off on a journey to build their own business is *fear*. "What if it doesn't work?" "What if I'm not good at it?" Fear—and the self-limiting beliefs that come with it—has a real power to hold people back.

It's not that fear doesn't come from something real. Ian Lawton teaches that fear is the memory of danger and serves a purpose by keeping us safe by telling us important things, like "Don't touch that red-hot stovetop!"

But in the business world, and really in the modern world overall, fear is becoming a dinosaur. That "fight or flight" response is a hangover from ancient times when people had to avoid flying spears and hungry mammoths. Back then, you often needed to act before thinking. And while life doesn't hold the same dangers for most of us now, fear still produces the same response in our brains. A message to run... or die! This message isn't really applicable in the business world.

That's why I try to separate healthy fear from unhealthy fear. I think of it as "photoshopping" my memories by updating the information and reframing the challenges that scare me. This puts me in the driver's seat and allows me to change my own mind by reframing a belief of "cannot" into "can do."

Which reminds me of another big inspiration: Roger Bannister. Back in 1954, scientists believed that it wasn't possible for a man to run a mile in four minutes. They thought the human body would actually break down at that speed! Roger, then a 25-year-old university student studying medicine, resolved to prove them wrong. People were so sure he would actually die in the attempt that doctors were on standby with oxygen, and reporters were ready to bring the story to the world when he ran his race.

But he completed the mile in 3.59 seconds and changed the world, not only because of the race itself but because of the realization that there was no need for the self-limiting belief that held so many runners back. In fact, within a month, Australian John Landry had broken the four-minute mile; within a year, hundreds had; proving that it just takes one person to believe they can achieve and in doing so, change the world.

Maybe that's why, any time I feel like giving up, I go back to those phrases, quotes, parables, movies, poems and inspiring stories of people who had been great leaders or achieved greatness in some way. Maybe some of my resolve comes from being British by birth—when I went to school most of the maps were pink, which meant "under British rule." I'm still inspired by Winston Churchill and the many millions of courageous people who risked their lives in global conflicts so we could have a better life.

DEALING WITH RISK

In business, we luckily don't have to risk our lives, but we still have to risk. The *Oxford English Dictionary* defines risk as "the exposure to the possibility of loss, injury, or other adverse or unwelcome circumstance; a chance or situation involving such a possibility." In business, you can't avoid risk, but you can (and should) assess each risk against the potential gain.

In my business and coaching practice, I help people avoid unnecessary risk by providing proven processes and best practices for a fast and successful start-up. As for becoming more comfortable with the risks you'll have to take, my advice is to build credibility early to help grow your confidence and remove self-limiting beliefs. I advise my clients to blog and write articles about what they know and to enter contests and competitions. I know, you're probably wondering how a relative newcomer to a field can muster up the nerve to enter a competition. The reality is, it's not all about winning—just filling out the entry form forces you to look at what you've achieved and where you want your business to go.

I've only recently learned how much this can mean. In January 2012, the Real Estate Staging Association gave out their very first Life-Time Achievement Award— and I was the recipient! When the president of the association, Shell Brodnax, called my name, you could have knocked me down with a feather! This was acknowledgement of the highest order, and even when I thought people weren't noticing, watching or cared, they were indeed.

It never would have happened if I had given up on my dream. So I'll leave you with the one quote that has inspired me the most over the years—a quote that's not from a business leader at all, but from the great Mother Teresa:

"People are often unreasonable, irrational, and self-centered. Forgive them anyway.

If you're kind, people may accuse you of selfish, ulterior motives. Be kind anyway.

If you are successful, you'll win some unfaithful friends and some genuine enemies. Succeed anyway.

If you're honest and sincere, people may deceive you. Be honest and sincere anyway.

What you spend years creating what others could destroy overnight. Create anyway.

If you find serenity and happiness, some may be jealous. Be happy anyway.

The good you do today will often be forgotten. Do good anyway.

Give the world the best you have, and it will never be enough. Give your best anyway.

In the final analysis, it's between you and God. It was never between you and them anyway."

Carpe diem!

About Christine

Christine Rae is known as the leading expert and trendsetter of the Real Estate Staging Industry. In her role as President and CEO for CSP® International, she steered the company to the top of the excellence chart for her industry. The CSP® International Academy is known as a successful incubator for would-be entrepreneurs with a decorating flair who want control over their own destiny, while building successful, profitable businesses of their own. CSP® International provides a safe haven for learning, support, knowledge, best practices and leading market trends. Graduates from the Academy benefit from a reputation of excellence, helping them gain credibility and recognition as they market and develop their own business.

Christine is recognized as the world's leading authority on staging from her global experience, as well as through her work in developing standards, examinations, professionalism and trend forecasting. She is the author of *Home Staging for Dummies*® (Wiley), editor of the world's only Staging Industry Magazine, and is co-author of *Sold, The Best Business Book You Will Ever Need*, and *Trendsetters.*

Christine developed and trademarked EcoStaging®. She is an Industry Expert Blogger for *REALTOR*® magazine, a regular contributor to *Real Estate* Magazine and is the Green Staging Expert for *HomeGain*®. She has been a featured speaker and keynote for many industry events, including six Stagers Expo's; Real Estate Staging Association; Sydney, Australia, Real Estate event; and expert speaker at the California Association of Realtors convention. Christine and her unique, signature CSP® Real Estate Staging Business Program has received awards, accolades, and recognition, including accreditation by RESA. In January 2012, she was presented with the prestigious Lifetime Achievement award from the Real Estate Staging Association for her work and contributions to the industry.

Currently five US colleges across the country endorse the program. Her book, *Home Staging for Dummies*®, has also been selected as the textbook on staging at several colleges in Canada.

Christine's success stems from her work ethic, desire for excellence, integrity and integral goodness. In a very competitive industry, what sets CSP® apart are the differentiators and the driving force to be of service and value to the student. From the outset, CSP® International core values, mission, "pay it forward" philosophy and their apprenticeship program have been the catalyst for the myriad of differentiators that set CSP® apart.

Christine has worked with TV House Doctor Ann Maurice. Many of Christine's graduates have appeared on popular HGTV real estate shows. She was recently certified to facilitate Michael E. Gerber's "Dreaming Room" event, was interviewed by Michael, and had a guest appearance on The Michael E. Gerber Show. She also has appeared on ABC, NBC, CBS and FOX television affiliates, speaking about staging.

www.StagingTrainging.com

CHAPTER 16

Healthy REALationships: Create, Maintain and Sustain Successful, Lucrative *Real* Relationships

By Andrea Adams-Miller

When it comes to total business and personal success, there are three beneficial secrets to generate success for the long term: creating, maintaining, and sustaining *"real"* relationships. Since you're reading this, it is obvious that you're smart, invested, and experienced enough to know there's a real art to *"real"* relationships. Likely, you want to develop these skills to increase your connections, your support, and your profitability. Fortunately, you probably recognize that, too often, businessmen and women seek a plethora of new contacts, hoping to attract a new client or a new referral; however, many of these businesspeople may be overlooking the key secrets of successful relationship building. They may not realize that they need more than a mass group of contacts to be successful. Business people need a skill set to attract the *right type* of people; otherwise, they're most likely wasting their time and the other people's time.

In reading this, you're likely aware that successful businesspeople need to invest in maintaining relationships if they want to go beyond an initial sale or a one-shot referral. Additionally, you're probably observant enough to notice that some of these businesspeople may not realize that a long-term *"real"* relationship is actually more lucrative then a collection of casual acquaintances or a mass collection of business cards. In their naivety, they may miss the mark in creating "REAL" relationships. Because of your intelligence, you know you want to avoid your peer's mistakes, and you want to know the secrets of those who have mastered the art of creating, maintaining, and sustaining lucrative "real" relationships.

ATTRACT THE RIGHT CLIENTS, PARTNERS, EMPLOYEES, VENDORS AND STAKEHOLDERS

Businesses invest an exorbitant amount of time and energy determining how to attract customers, partners, employees, vendors and stakeholders (from here out referred to as "clients") through research. However, before the research is conducted to attract the customer, business owners and leaders need to determine the key secret to determining who the right customer is for them. Fortunately, finding the magic formula for client attraction doesn't have to be time consuming, difficult, or challenging. Simply put, ask yourself, "What type of client do I want?" If you're struggling with determining what kind of client you want, then invest in the right consultant who can quickly and easily show you how you can map your key desires for clientele. Once the client has been identified, then you may need to restructure what you offer to make sure your message, brand, and products match the type of client for which you're looking. When you know who your clients are, then it's easier to go where they congregate to connect with them as well as to build a "real" relationship with them. Once you do these simple things, you can attract the "right" customers.

As an example, over the last 15 years, my business—"Healthy REALationships," www.IgniteYourRelationships.com—has changed and evolved as the business reached different levels of success. After realizing our clients' desires for us to expand our services beyond improving interpersonal relationships, we were encouraged to realize our business potential, based on our knowledge, research and experience. Ultimately, we realized that our clients wanted us to expand our business model to include consulting services for business relationships so they could reach higher levels of success in their professional careers, too.

Fortunately, we had clients who were willing to ask for what they wanted. Still, we learned that the hard way. We were like every other business when expanding, jumping in with both feet, struggling to learn the path to success, and missing the mark! Fortunately, someone told me, "Hey, Andrea! You're wagging the dog by the tail!" What he meant was that I created a business expansion based on what I *thought* my customers *needed,* but I didn't know *who* all these clients were, nor did I really know *what* they *wanted.* I can laugh now knowing if I would have only had the foresight to *identify* my client pool first, then go out and meet my potential clients where they were, then I could develop a *real* relationship with these wonderful people. If I would have discovered these secrets 16 years ago, my business could have excelled exponentially in my first years, rather than forcing me to struggle to learn the secrets. If only we would have known these secrets then, or known a company like ours that would have been able to guide us through these steps so we could have quickly and easily mastered the secrets from the beginning! While we can't go back and take that struggle away, we can share what we have learned so you *don't* have to *struggle* or *work hard* to attract the *right* clients, partners, employees, vendors and stakeholders.

RELATIONSHIPS DON'T GET BETTER THE HARDER YOU WORK ON THEM!

Speaking of working hard, we've all been told a lie! We've been repetitively told by well-intentioned businesspeople, religious leaders, parents, and mentors that working hard on your relationships will make them more successful! It's not true, and please know it's not your fault that you've been listening all these years, wondering how come the rewards, income and freedom have never come to fruition as promised. Our leaders thought they we doing us a favor, when, in fact, we now know that they were doing us a disservice! We have since learned at www.IgniteYourRelationships.com that when it comes to work, we need to work *right*; however, when it comes to relationships, we need to *stop working hard* and *start playing hard*.

Let me clarify "play." In the literal term, "play" constitutes amusement from an activity; however, when play is defined according to psychological measures, play brings about positive social, behavioral and psychological factors. Therefore, when I started increasing the amount of deliberate activities, conversations, and behaviors that parallel *play* as a positive factor, as CEO and founder of "Healthy REALationships," I found that all my relationships, personal and professional, deepened.

I knew more about the people I worked with and partnered with in business than ever before. Additionally, they came to know me better, too, adding to the knowledge that if people *know* you, they will trust you and invest in you! As a result, the deeper or the more "real" our relationships became, the more these clients, partners, employees, vendors, and stakeholders invested in me, our products, and in our business. When I think back at how our business started, and how hard I *struggled and worked* at creating, maintaining, and sustaining relationships compared to now that I build relationships by focusing on connecting through social, behavioral and psychological "play," the relationships come so much easier.

Don't be like I was: Don't attempt to reinvent the wheel, wag the dog by the tail, and waste considerable time and energy. You don't have to *work hard* at your relationships anymore, *work right* and *play hard* by investing in time with a consultant or consulting business. The *right* consultant can reveal the secrets to *playing hard* and show you the secrets to overcome the myth of hard work you've been led to believe all these years!

PUTTING SIZZLE IN BUSINESS RELATIONSHIPS IS AS EASY AS BUTTER ON A HOT SKILLET

Now that you've learned the secret to attracting the right business clients, partners, vendors and stakeholders, and now that you know how to maintain these REAL relationships, it's time to learn how to turn up the heat! This is where many businesses fail in sustaining relationships. Some businesses and entrepreneurs just don't get that once you have the client, you have a hot skillet already; these connections are already interested in you and what you have to offer. Yet, businesses fail to offer these clients, partners, employees, vendors and stakeholders the opportunity to take their business relationships with you to a higher level.

If you've already attracted the right client and maintained a "REAL" relationship, then all you have to do is offer them the time, the product, the opportunity, the ticket, or the investment deal for them to want to be a part of something greater. If you've done your homework and are offering them something of great value combined with a fantastic opportunity, then there's no reason for you or them to hold back! We are a society of *"I Want It and I Want It Now"*—we want more, and we know we can have it, even if we have to buy it. Therefore, your clients are just waiting for someone like you or your business to offer what they want to them! Now's the time, so stroke their business erogenous zones! Find out what makes their pulse race—more money, more clients, more joint ventures or more publicity. Find out what makes them hot to do business with you, then structure the system or opportunity for them to take it. Once you've mastered one area, it's a normal pathway for partners in a *real* relationship to seek a higher commitment, an even deeper connection to explore new territory.

For example, after revealing interpersonal relationship secrets to a particular client, they asked me to help them reduce their money problems as money, or lack thereof, was interfering with intimacy. These clients literally said, *"Andrea, your business is really successful. Tell us your secrets on how you increased your business success."* So I turned up the heat, spending a portion of their consulting time on how to turn their business around to be more financially lucrative. When I gave them advice that doubled their yearly income after one session, they were hooked. The faith they now had in me, the relief they had from financial burden, and the fun they had in their personal life all increased. It led me to offer this service to all my clients. By turning up the heat for them by increasing their business and interpersonal happiness, I rejuvenated the productivity in my own business as I realized how turning up the heat for them was now something valuable for almost every client we had ever had who called for a consultation!

Again, some of you reading this may only need the permission to forge ahead, yet others need that added value of guidance from someone who has been there before and mastered the pathway. If so, then don't hesitate to invest in a consulting business that understands where you've been and where you're going. If you study the best of the best, those that are still doing business successfully, you'll see that they, too, still invest in continual personal and professional development with the help of a consultant or many consultants. Why *work hard* by *working alone*, *work right* and *play hard* with someone who can *reveal* the secrets you *want* to achieve all you *dream, desire,* and frankly *deserve* for *creating, maintaining,* and *sustaining "real"* relationships that are *successful* and *lucrative for life!*

About Andrea

Andrea Adams-Miller, CEO and founder of "Healthy REALationships," www.IgniteYourRelationships.com, is a highly sought-after keynote speaker, relationship consultant, business consultant, author, columnist, and an international award-winning talk radio show host. Andrea Reveals the Secrets on Igniting the Spark, Fire, & Passion in Relationships to Create, Maintain, and Sustain "REAL" Relationships in Business and in your Personal Life to Secure a $uccessful, Lucrative Career and Happy, Satisfying Personal Relationships.

Audiences are amazed at Andrea's high-energy on stage and her genuine care for the betterment of their lives, their businesses, and their relationships. Clients appreciate her positive, no-nonsense, solutions-focused attitude that reflects through the Power of the 7 E's: experiential learning, empowerment, encouragement, engagement, enlightenment, energy, and entertainment. By using these qualities, Andrea ignites the spark, fire, and passion to build "real" relationships every time she speaks or consults!!

Because Andrea is fun, interesting, and easy to work with, she has been on numerous newspaper, radio, and television programs, such as PBS, CBS, NBC, ABC, FOX, 20/20, *TIME* magazine, *MORE* magazine, Gene Simmon's "Family Jewels," *E! Style, Business News Daily,* and *Web MD*. Andrea has spoken at the same events as well-known celebrities, such as Jack Canfield (author, *Chicken Soup for the Soul* Series), Stedman Graham (author, businessman, and Oprah's boyfriend), and Anthony Hopkins (Oscar Winning Actor), Jason Alexander (George Costanza from "Seinfeld"), James Malinchak (featured on ABC's "Secret Millionaire"), and more.

Andrea's vast knowledge and experience in relationship and business consulting over the last 15 years puts her at the forefront of her field. Therefore, she consults with people from around the world via the internet. Andrea also offers consultation face-to-face at the client's location or at her private office in her hometown of Findlay, Ohio, or from her satellite office in Vegas.

Prior to her career as a keynote speaker, she worked in the law enforcement field, and then opened a relationship consulting business. She teaches college academia in the fields of business, psychology, sociology, law enforcement, criminal justice, communications and health professions. Andrea has earned her Master of Science in Public Health Community Education and Health Promotion, and she's writing her dissertation in the same field. She and her husband, entrepreneur Tom Miller, have three beautiful daughters; her youngest, Demiya Miller, is an author with her own business, www.TeenStudentSuccess.com. All of Andrea's life experiences, education and research have helped her become the well-rounded, well-educated and joyful person she is today.

To sign up for her *free* Newsletter Special Report Series *"REALationships: The 7 Essential E's to Igniting 'Real' Relationships,"* visit www.IgniteYourRelationships.com to reserve your copy. Or call (419) 722-6931 to book Andrea Adams-Miller for your next event or consultation, so she can share with you and your audience the secrets to create, maintain and sustain *"real"* successful and lucrative relationships!

CHAPTER 17

Using Your Innate DNA Success Gene to Achieve Profit

By Asara Lovejoy, author of *The One Command*

To know that we know what we know, and to know that we do not know what we do not know, that is true knowledge. —Copernicus

The other day I had a very successful businessman tell me an important story about his business. He was an investment expert and had clients who invested $2 to $3 million at a time with him. He came to me because he said, "I'm stuck Asara, and I want to go beyond my own ceiling."

I asked, "What would you like?"

He replied, "To speak to investors that invest $30 million or more with me."

"What stands in your way," I questioned.

"I don't feel qualified to speak to them," he said.

I told him that seemed humorous to me that he could elicit $3 million but not $30 million and that he had a self-inflicted barrier against the larger sum. As his coach I said, "Let's get down to work."

"What is the reason, in your mind, that you have reached your ceiling and can't go any higher," I asked.

He replied, "In my family we were taught to be very humble. Admittedly $3 million may not seem humble to some, but $30 million seems to be excessive, rude, impolite."

I suggested that his mind-set and his idea of politeness could change, if he was willing to let it change.

"Yes, yes, Asara I definitely want it to change."

This little conversation exemplifies the first two essential truths for change. The first is to be *willing to identify the current mind-set* that's causing your ceiling or limits, and to identify it honestly without judgment against yourself or your conditions. It feels impolite and excessive is an honest assessment.

The second is to have the *courage to ask for change*. Here's where it gets interesting. I know you've heard that you can't solve a problem or create new money or wealth or solve a financial dilemma from the same place in your mind that the problem first developed. Yet most people try to problem-solve in their ordinary beta, logical-thinking mind 98 percent of the time, with only a 1 percent return.

I discovered through my studies and the mentors who directed me to the science of thought and theories of the quantum field that each and every one of us—yes, that means you—is biologically hard-wired for success. Each one has a success gene and a super-intelligence that's personally yours.

This super-intelligence isn't found in your logical-thinking fast brain wave of your everyday problem-solving processor. It has been identified in science as your theta brain wave. I'll talk more about how to easily access your theta mind, but right now let me share the benefits. When you slow your brain to theta, something powerful happens in problem-solving, or to break out of a profit barrier. You simply let go, thinking that you have to have the answer, or if you "just work hard enough," you'll find it. Instead you tap into an open potential of a new answer—one you may never ever be able to find with your logical mind. An answer that does exist but resides in another portion of your intelligence.

You already use this profit-generating part of your mind. If you've ever gone to bed to sleep on a problem and woke up with the answer, or if you've ever had an epiphany, an "ah-ha" moment, then you found that answer from your theta mind and your greater intelligence.

What would it be like to establish an on-demand system to solve problems, break out of limits, and create new profits in your business success? We know the answer—it would be fantastic!

The third essential truth is that once you've identified your current mind-set and acted with the courage to ask for a change, *you then identify what it is you want instead.* For example, "I want $30 million investors."

Most folks, even if they make it this far, are stopped here. They stop here because the self-imposed limits rise up, such as the thought that it's impossible or how would I do that, or it can't be done anyway.

The beauty of your innate DNA success gene is that it can find an answer if you get your thinking out of the way. Start with, "I don't know how." This relaxes your body and your stress level because you're telling the truth—you truly don't know how in this moment. (In our culture we, unfortunately, have this 10-second rule—know the answer immediately or else, but this mind-set releases us from that stressor.)

This is the first phase of finding an answer to take your profit to the next level.

This is the musing stage. I don't know the answer. I don't know the form. I don't know how to take my business or my life to the next level. In the musing stage, let yourself hang out with not knowing for a while. This stops your reactive mind that wants to flare up the negative doomsday predictions.

The next phase is to consciously access your greater mind. In *The One Command,* I teach an easy six-step process that quickly takes you into theta, but for now you can change from one mind-set to the other by changing your physiology.

Imagine you're fully present in your body, then roll your eyes up under your closed eyelids and think for a moment—"I'm open to an answer." The physical movement of your eyes looking up under your closed eyelids physically changes your brain wave from fast, impatient demanding beta to open potential theta state.

You may not have known up until now that you have a powerhouse of knowledge with answers to problems, the ability to stop negative thoughts, and to ask for what you want through a physical process, but you do and it produces fantastic results.

There are qualities of thought that are found in your theta/delta brain wave that don't exist in your beta thinking—ordinary consciousness of limited thought that operates in duality of this or that, yes or no, maybe, maybe not. In addition, beta mind looks to the past and projects the past into the future, re-creating the same thought template again and again with the same limited results.

You cannot solve a problem or create new money or wealth, or solve a financial dilemma from the same place in your mind that the problem developed. As I said earlier, most people try to problem-solve in their ordinary beta mind 98 percent of the time, with a 1 percent return causing repetitive limits.

An unlimited potential exists in the theta/delta frequencies of your thought. Here your mind perceives reality in a unified field of now, with no past to draw upon or future to imagine—only unlimited ideas and potentials to create. Here you think in a state of peace, joy, security and inventiveness, as solutions arrive in unimaginable ways, all within a deeper connection within your heart and mind. For a 1 percent moment of concentration in theta, you get 100 percent return of your time and energy.

You get that result, because as you command a thought in theta, you physically and biologically interrupt all the thoughts that derail that truth at the same time you simultaneously create a new DNA blueprint for that thought to appear in physical form. You're hard-wired with the ability to accomplish this.

In a moment of physically changing your eye focus to look up under your closed eyelids, you can mechanically shift your beta mind into theta mind and engage those portions of your intelligence that are ready, willing and able to be engaged by you at this very moment.

The theta brain wave has some unique and powerful properties. First, it's the place where you go into deep rapid eye movement (REM) sleep at least three times a night. Next, while in REM sleep, you discharge negative thoughts and fears from the day and from the past. You also create what you dream to be realized in making your hopes, wishes and desires come true.

The theta/delta slow brain-wave frequencies heal the body, engage directly with your cells and your DNA, and establish neurological pathways for thought—your belief system and your habit of thought. By directly accessing this fantastic powerhouse of reality, you can consciously change the direction of your life by choice, and you can do all this in a moment.

There is a process of change that takes place as you delink your old synaptic pathways of thought and create new DNA blueprints of reality. This process of change is a physical, emotional event. Let's say you're frustrated with your profits at the moment. Here again are the A, B, C's of making a change in your beliefs about your present state.

A. Identify your fears and thoughts about your net profits. There are a variety of reasons you can come up with: The economy is poor, I don't have enough education, my family has always been middle class or poor and I can't go any higher than them, being rich and successful will make me a bad person, and so forth.

B. Identify what it is that you want instead. For example: I want to increase my profits right now in this economy, I can be rich and a good person, my quality of thought and intelligence are more important than my level of education. As you can see, the process is to claim that which you truly want to believe but don't think you do at this moment.

C. Now that you know what you truly want, in my system of change you would go through the six steps to engage in theta but right now make a state change by looking up under your closed eyes and command a change in your thinking.

Coherence in your body, mind and emotions now takes place. As you stop your old idea of limitation by commanding what you want instead while in theta, a new blueprint is created in your DNA. In this new blueprint you have no past and no future. You only have *the now of this event* that you created. Faith and trust are required in this moment because even as you have made a change, there's no physical evidence of that change yet.

Some of the symptoms of change you experience after making a command in theta are feeling relaxed and peaceful about what you want—more income, reduced debt, a better-paying job or career. Your body and mind have to come to a new understanding that's relaxed and peaceful rather than fearful and stressed.

You'll be amazed at how quickly you can get used to making change in this way, especially when you see the results materialize.

One woman who was a personal assistant for a high-powered boss in a rich company thought it would be great to get a bonus from her boss, even though a bonus for her position had never happened in the lifetime of the company. She and I had a coaching session to identify her limited, fearful thoughts and to establish what she wanted instead. We then went through the six-step process and commanded for her generous bonus.

Later, she called with the best news and the most familiar statement I hear, "Asara, you won't believe what happened." I reply, "Yes I will." She said, "I just got a check for a $10,000 bonus from my boss in recognition of my above-the-line contribution to him and the business. Imagine that." This was the exact amount she had commanded to appear.

There are a couple of ideas that you want to focus on when beginning this next mastery of your life.

- One is that you have the power to create new realities—all the time.

- Next, you must meet yourself exactly where you are, with no judgment against what you've done in the past or what you may do while creating new results.

- You must also give yourself permission to be in the perfection of your current experience, and from your current experience, you define new roads to travel and new paths to climb, remembering the formula of telling the truth about your judgments and fears and replacing them with what you want instead.

Eventually the threshold of your new state stabilizes as you develop new habits of thought in all portions of your brain, mind and body—from the frontal lobe images and imagination to the chemical activity of firing a thought. Eventually, you live the essence of your true self that deploys a greater good and service

Getting back to the story, my client and I continued the process to command a change in theta for his $30 million investors. We changed the idea that it was impolite to be in business with that higher level of wealth. We did it in such a way that he was in harmony and congruent about doing business in a larger arena. I can still be humble he said because I am a humble man, and each person I do business with is someone with whom I have a relationship, not with the money but the person.

Ahhhhh…What a nice, new idea. He called me the following week to say he had his first $30 million investor.

Thank you for sharing some of your valuable time with me by reading my chapter. I have a special gift waiting for you at www.bookguide-asara.com that takes you right through the Six-Step and One Command process where you can quickly try out what you discovered here.

You can also visit www.onecommandlife.com and www.commandingwealth.com to learn more and continue the adventure.

To reach Asara Lovejoy, directly email info@commandingwealth.com or call (855) 862-463 (TOC-INFO). The office will quickly reply.

About Asara

Asara Lovejoy, bestselling author of *The One Command* and president and founder of The One Command Global Corp., has touched millions of lives in her Clear Channel radio career and thousands more as a speaker, keynote presenter and trainer worldwide. Asara says, "I get to live my highest values of awakened consciousness and transformation every day. In that moment of my own down-and-out loss, not only did I receive the content of an understanding of living life differently as shared in *The One Command*, but by applying those very principles I went from nearly broke to generating more than $2 million in revenue (and still growing). This growth came, not from a material product that's easy to value but an intangible idea. My greatest joy is seeing the lives of individuals change dramatically for the better and seeing business owners and entrepreneurs develop revenue and profits in a completely new way, with the power of their minds.

Since publishing the book, a wave of requests for more information reaches The One Command organization every day. We've been in direct contact with more than 300,000 individuals (growing daily) who love *The One Command* and want to apply it for change in their life.

Here are some ways you can find out more and receive support for making the changes you want:

First, please go to www.bookguide.asara.com and immediately receive your gifts from us as our way of saying thank you. You'll get the MP3 guided meditation to go through the six steps and make your Command, a PDF of the six steps to print, our very popular MP3 "Six Steps to Mastering The One Command," and the complete "Meet The One Command Program." Wow, that's a lot, and I think you'll enjoy the material!

We also have a large worldwide One Command community where you can ask questions, be supported, and learn more with daily One Command messages that inspire, uplift and encourage. You'll find us at www.onecommandlife.com. In addition, you'll find great articles, blogs and much more.

Visit all our websites as each one is rich in content with specific information.

See you there!

www.bookguide-asara.com
www.onecommandlife.com
www.asara.com
www.commandingwealth.com
For direct contact, you can email us at clientcare@commandingwealth.com or call (855) 862-4636 (TOC-INFO).

CHAPTER 18

Design Your Life, Live Your Dreams

By Katie Joy, "The Global Butterfly"

You know how there's always one or two (maybe more) truly defining moments in your life that give you a wake-up call to what it is you really want?

Well, perhaps my first burning desire to consciously design my life, to live my dreams, was during an incident when I was just 16 years old in 1996.

My family of two parents, two younger brothers and I lived, as most Australians do, paycheck to paycheck. But in our case, as Dad was rather entrepreneurial, it had been a roller coaster ride of some money coming in, then periods of drought. My dad was always working hard—and stressed. I hardly spent much time with my dad. And when he was around, he was often grumpy, stressed, and sometimes often seemingly angry at life.

We always had enough money for the essentials, and even sometimes enough for some small family treats, such as outings or takeout food. But I often felt angry and disappointed, not just at feeling the stress of a lack of money for the extracurricular activities I wanted to do (such as going on my high school ski trip) but because there was always tension around money, and it seemingly being the reason for the family disconnect.

While I now have a great relationship with my father, this one particular day when I was 16, I'd just had a standing row with my dad where I was vying for his attention. He was busy handling life, business, his own emotions, and stories, and looking back—the poor man could hardly breathe. During the heated moment, out of frustration, he backhanded me. Shocked and angry, I cried, "I will never be broke or poor! I will be wildly wealthy!"

That moment has stuck with me ever since. Little did I know how much that experience had permeated my conscious and subconscious, as my story will reveal.

What I wanted most at the time with my father was attention, approval and love, but most of all, quality family time. You know, those simple things that make us feel valuable and loved.

These values of quality time and family still rate as some of my highest core values, along with adventure, fun, learning, financial freedom, laughing, being playful, enjoying life, exploring and discovering new experiences.

It's these core values that have been my driving force to create a vision for my life, to live it on purpose, and consciously design it to my own blueprint.

As I grew up, I watched so many people in my life be buffered around in the "storms" of life and by what other people think, because they had never set the coordinates for their own direction, or decided what they wanted their life to be about.

While I've always set high intentions and visions for my life, it's still been an incredible journey of ups and downs, but all the situations are great gifts to refine my vision and decide what I really want, and what's no longer serving me, so I can now let go of it.

Moving forward from my teenage years, I ended up choosing to get married during my 20s, twice! Both marriages ended in divorce but not without their lessons. While there were some great times, the greatest challenge that brought me the greatest gift is that both the men I chose to marry (at different times) were challenged financially. This felt like *déjà vu,* but I soon discovered in coming years that the subconscious driving force within me was looking to "fix" a man financially, so therefore I would be worthy of his love. This all looped back to that defining incident with my dad when I was a teenager, seeking his attention, love and approval.

Once I became aware that my common denominating factor was my own source of learning a life lesson, I decided I didn't need *that* lesson anymore, and set my vision for my life to be abundant with wealth, not only financially but with time freedom, to do the things I really wanted to do, spend the time with the people I really wanted to spend time with, and focus my energies on learning, serving and growing as best I could.

So with an early interest in property from my teenage years (my dad was a carpenter/builder by trade) and later discovering a transformational book for my life called *Rich Dad, Poor Dad,* by Robert Kyosaki, I began studying real estate through-out my 20s.

I would read magazines and books by people who had made money through property. I also read many books on debt management and how to create wealth.

Probably the most fundamental of all, though, I began creating a vision of being debt-free, wealthy, traveling the world, enjoying life, being fit and healthy, enjoying time at home cooking for family and friends, spending quality time with loved ones, learning and exploring fields of interest to me.

I knew from a young age that I wanted to have my life be more than simply going to work, having a good job, having the typical Aussie home with a fat mortgage to pay into my 50s or 60s, etc. It simply didn't appeal to me, as most people seemed so dissatisfied and stressed.

I wanted more out of life!

So I began by creating more in my mind's eye first. I began to visualize.

I loved to read, and in the beginning of my financial journey, books were all I could afford. I bought *Think and Grow Rich* by Napoleon Hill. That became a game-changer for me. I read the book, highlighting it like mad to pluck out the key lessons. And I implemented what I learned immediately.

By the time I was 32, I had been through two marriages (and debt management through to wealth) and several careers (mostly as a personal trainer, then later as a paramedic), using my income to invest in positive cash flow property, moving me toward my ideal vision in my mind's eye of how I wanted to create my life with financial and time freedom.

In March 2008, I had met my financial goals of replacing my working income with passive income. So I retired as a paramedic and began living my dream lifestyle of traveling the world and exploring (so far, seven continents and 52 countries from 2008 to 2012).

The irony is that as soon as I leveraged myself even more and got out of my own way, my passive income tripled along with my net worth continuously growing, even though I was traveling and only focused my energies on "working" perhaps four hours a month!

All because I had developed and implemented the skills for wealth and lifestyle-design creation, and had created massive momentum.

I put my energies during these past four years into developing me, exploring the world, seeking out great coaches and being mentored by masters. I enrolled in my own "University of Life, which has expanded my world and opened so many possibilities that have far exceeded my imagination.

Among many incredible experiences, I've had opportunities to ice-mountain climb in Antarctica, go on safari in Africa, travel many states within America, explore the Peruvian Amazon and Machu Pichu, cruise the Caribbean, travel throughout Europe, and even spend a week on Necker Island with my No. 1 mentor, Sir Richard Branson!

While the vehicle I chose to create my financial wealth was predominantly property (I also later created additional streams of income through online business and book royalties), it was the focus of having a clear vision for my life that fueled my daily actions to overcome the challenges, get up when I felt tired, and inspired me when I'd been working 20 hour days and needed to still keep going to manifest my goals.

What made my life for me was my decision to define my own life. To define my own purpose (and giving myself permission to change the purpose but always having a purpose). I claimed my own destiny. I knew that if I didn't choose what it would look like for myself, that I'd end up like most everyone else in my life at the time—being defined by other people's decisions of what my life should look and be like.

I thank my own spirit every day for being rebellious and listening to my own inner voice.

So often I get asked, *"How did you design your life to live your dreams?"* So here are 12 fundamental things you might want to consider (and take action on) to consciously design your life to live your dreams:

1. **Create a physical vision board.** What do you really want in each area of your life? Where do you want to live? What do you want to do with your time? Who do you want to spend time with regularly? What do you want to learn? How do you want to contribute? These are just some of the key questions you might want to ask yourself to begin to consciously design your own lifestyle blueprint. Once created, keep your vision board in daily view and update accordingly.

2. **Write your own bucket list.** This is a list of items, experiences, people you want to meet, things you want to learn, etc. during your lifetime. This is a fundamental way to let yourself be a kid again and stretch your imagination to write down what you want your life to be about.

3. **Know (choose) your core highest values,** and define winning rules for you to experience these highest values easily, accessibly and daily!

4. **Decide on clear S.M.A.R.T.Y goals in alignment with your vision and values.** Specific, Measurable, Attainable, Realistic, Timely and whY (you want them).

5. **Develop yourself.** Read daily. Jim Rohn is famous for saying, *"Invest more in yourself than you do in your business."* (Sometimes interpreted as job or career). The more you grow *you,* the greater success you will have with business, finance, life, relationships, etc.

6. **Be grateful, meditate and visualize daily your outcomes as if they're already done.** Future-pace experiencing your life with your goals already achieved. Feel grateful for *all* of it, including the journey and experiences you are about to go through to achieve your outcomes.

7. **Model success, which means finding people who walk their talk and have already done what it is you want to do in your life.** Read their stories (biographies, autobiographies, how to books, blogs, and even social media).

8. **Manage your mind-set.** Focusing on developing a winning attitude, being a problem solver, seeking the gifts and the best in life, being grateful, being generous, kind to yourself and others, using positive affirmations and deciding on using only empowering language to communicate with yourself and others.

9. **Get a coach** who will call you on your b.s., help you to redefine clarity within your life (or the areas you might have lost focus in), guide you along your path toward your goals, and help you hold yourself accountable to what it is you say that you want so you get *results!*

10. **Become a "money master" and educate yourself financially how to use money, so it doesn't use you!** Financial education isn't taught in school, unfortunately. But the system is set up to focus the educational attention on a job-mentality—J.O.B = Just Over Broke. To become wealthy, you must do what the wealthy do. Develop your mind-set and financial acuity to learn the fundamental principles and skills of managing money so you can grow your wealth. Money won't mean you have a problem-free life (often the problems get bigger as you grow bigger), but it will give you a lot more choices.

11. **Be organized, and develop the daily discipline of this habit.** As your wealth and life grows, you'll need to be systemized to break through ceilings that otherwise would cap you, because you're amidst chaos. Being systematized frees up your thoughts and energy to be even more creative and leverage your life so you can do more of what you really want to do, instead of being bogged down in doing everything yourself or doing repetitive tasks. Being organized helps with outsourcing to others what it is you need them to do.

12. **Delegate.** Focus on what your strengths are; forget trying to strengthen your weak areas. Match yourself with other people who can compliment you with their strengths and free up your

energy for being great at your own genius. Allow others to do the same. This authentic living also frees up your energy to enjoy life and your journey a whole lot more. Don't mistake *busyness* for *business*. Take massive effective action, without mistaking movement for achievement. You can get much more stuff done in quality time and have more free time by being clear on your outcomes and delegating much of the tasks or projects that aren't your greatest strengths so you can put your energy and time into quality areas that are going to make you more money and produce even greater results. Building a quality team around you will create abundance for all and leverage your business so you can have a life!

Bonus Tip: **Communication with yourself first and foremost is a key fundamental.** Being kind, self-praising, supportive and encouraging, essentially being your own raving fan. It doesn't mean you're full of yourself or lack humility. In fact, it means that you love yourself to care for you first. When this is done with a genuine heart, it will also reflect on how you communicate and treat others also. Constantly working on your communication skills (language, listening, speaking, etc) will be a fundamental asset to your success. [1]

Notes

1. © Katie Joy www.TheGlobalButterfly.com 2012. All Rights Reserved.

About Katie

Katie Joy is a globetrotter, travelling the world sprinkling her magic wherever she goes, breathing life and enthusiasm into those she meets with her enlightened perspectives, personal experiences, sense of candid humor, and educating with practical steps to create the life of your dreams. She energizes people into action with her effervescent joy. Her vivacious yet grounded presence brings forth teachings with fun, laughter, joy and new insights to see the gifts each person has in life. Her exceptional view of life, philosophy and enlightened understanding of how to create life on your own terms is transforming the lives of millions. As a researcher, writer, speaker, life coach, philosopher and retired paramedic, her studies and life experiences have made her a leading expert on how to consciously create your ideal lifestyle by design, healing, human potential and philosophy.

Katie retired in 2008 at age 32. She's been traveling the world full time since, visiting some of the most exotic and sometimes adventurous spots in the world, and hanging out with some of the biggest movers and shakers. A self-made millionaire, twice over, Katie lives the life of her dreams with those she loves. It's a remarkable life!

Get your _Free Gift_ from Katie Joy:

How to Create Your Vision Board to Get Results e-book and bonus video *(valued at $97)* at www.TheGlobalButterfly.com/nbnvbgift

CHAPTER 19

To Improve Your Business, Family and Personal Success, Do What Your Momma Said

By Patti Thor

Would you like to know the secret used to turn a bumbling startup business into more than $14 million per year within five years, with new customers coming 100 percent from referrals? This same secret tool can turn a subpar employee around, improve your family life, even help you lose weight. And most likely your momma taught you this when you were a child. Interested?

Tom Hopkins, a former construction worker, decided to step up into a business that had unlimited potential for success. At age 19, he chose real estate. He tried applying for real estate jobs on his way home from his day job, still dressed in his construction clothes. One broker decided to give Tom a chance but told him he needed to wear a suit. Having only his old band uniform, he showed up wearing it to sell real estate and make his fortune. Tom's boss laughed and said that if this kid could make it, everyone else in the firm should be rich. Tom was undeterred by a less than rousing start; his first six months of business had sales averaging $42 per month. Clearly, this wouldn't support him and his young family. But he had a passion for real estate and learned that he needed to build relationships to increase sales. So he started with a secret tool: gratitude.

Every day Tom sent 10 thank-you notes. His list included customers, friends, prospects and new acquaintances. On Tom's end, that forced him to get the names and addresses of people every day. The recipients, for their part, appreciated Tom thinking highly enough of them to handwrite a note of gratitude. After only three years in real estate, Tom's business was 100 percent referrals! He worked as an agent for only six years. During his last year, he sold 365 homes—the equivalent of one each day. Tom wrapped up his career in real estate with a grand total of 1,553 transactions. Not bad for starting at $42 per month income in a band uniform.

"Everyone has an invisible sign hanging from their neck saying, "Make me feel important." Never forget this message when working with people." This is the philosophy of Mary Kay Ash, "the Queen of Gratitude."

Mary Kay taught her beauty consultants (sales staff) to thank their hostess (client) and compliment at least one thing about the hostess' home when entering to teach a skin-care class (demonstrate the products to a group of a client's referrals.) The words of thanks and the compliment formed a sense of gratitude in both the consultant and the hostess.

Ash was also famous for writing thank-you notes to consultants who performed well or even those who took the time to write to her. I remember getting a handwritten response from her when I was a new consultant. I went on to win many sales awards with the company.

Mary Kay set company policy with gratitude and praise as the foundation. Her top two goals in dealing with employees, customers, or family and friends were, first, to make every individual feel important and, second, to praise each one frequently and publicly—criticism or correction was relegated to a private setting and sandwiched between compliments.

Ash tried to regularly thank each representative for something that was true so that her gratitude came from the heart. She taught her supervisors that if they needed to give a warning to a subpar employee, then the supervisor needed to thank that employee *10* times for something he or she was doing right, before giving any corrections. Mary Kay told those leaders to watch what would happen. In most cases, no warning would be necessary; the employee began to improve in many areas and would self-correct.

Jack Mitchell is CEO of Mitchells/Richards/Marshs, the family-started luxury clothing stores, and author of *Hug Your Customers and Hug Your*

People. Mitchell says, "Giving great personalized customer service has always been the foremost goal in my family, but one thing we never lose sight of is you can't possibly deliver great service if you don't treat your own associates right." He adds, "Generously recognize them (and not only with money, but don't be chintzy, either)."

Another business leader who shows this kind of gratitude is James Malinchak. Years ago I was at a fundraiser for the Just Like My Child Foundation, where Malinchak gave a keynote. I sent him a short video to thank him for what I learned from him during his talk. I knew that he wasn't getting paid for giving the presentation yet was giving us his best stuff. There were a dozen other speakers to whom I also sent videos. However, James handwrote a thank-you note to me for his thank-you video. He didn't do this to garner recognition for himself but to recognize and encourage me. I've told this story to dozens, and now, via this book, to thousands. Gratitude is exponential—it multiplies itself.

The people whom Tom, Mary Kay, Jack and James had been thanking felt appreciated and important. Author of *Unlimited Referrals,* Bill Cates, explains, "Referrals come through who you are, not what you sell." I deduce from this statement that if you or your company makes me feel appreciated, then you would also treat my friends well. The contrary is also true: If you make me feel as if you don't care or that I am a bother, then I will not only fail to refer you but will, according to statistics, tell 5 to 10 times more people to steer clear of you than the number of those to whom I would recommend you.

Maya Angelou puts it this way, "I've learned that people will forget what you said, people will forget what you did, but people will never forget how you made them feel."

According to a study by the Rockefeller Corp., 68 percent of customers stop doing business with a company that they think doesn't care about them. And most never even tell the company. Why would they if they think the company doesn't care? Two other studies confirm that 70 to 73 percent leave for this same reason. Only 14 percent of customers leave due to product dissatisfaction, the second-ranked reason. The large gap between the top two reasons indicates that more people buy from you because of how *you* make them feel rather than how your *product* makes them feel. That's a difference that you have great control over. This same concept can be extended to your employee relations and your home life. (We'll get to that in a few paragraphs.)

London-based company Chiumento conducted their "Energising Business Research" study, in conjunction with *Personnel Today*. Their research showed that two-thirds of the workers surveyed believed that feeling appreciated and having their work recognized made them a lot more productive. A simple "thank you" from colleagues gave a much-needed boost in the workplace. All the workers felt at least some increase in productivity with the encouragement. Praise from management had the second biggest impact.

In the old TV show "Land of the Giants," the people had to work together to climb stairs. One person was lifted up and supported by the others as he worked to get to the next level. He would then reach back and help another person achieve that level and so on, until all were upgraded. This is a picture of gratitude in action. We must remember that we cannot climb any huge step by ourselves; it takes the dedication and support of others. Likewise, we will never be able to climb to a new level unless we reach back to those who helped us and uplift them, too. Gratitude is one of the simplest yet most powerful ways to boost another person.

Besides saying, "thank you," how can we offer gratitude? As humans, the sound we love most is our own name, as evidenced by our being able to hear it spoken from across a noisy room. The *attitude* that we love to receive most is gratitude—to be acknowledged, loved and appreciated. We each have a certain amount of insecurity and want to be assured that we are worthy.

To help meet this need in your business associates, establish the habit of gratitude. Each day tell your customers and employees that you are grateful for them and why. Name a specific attribute, action or accomplishment of theirs for which you are thankful. Remember to express gratitude to people outside of your work environment as well. This is vital to building the habit of gratefulness and establishing this trait in your character.

When we take time to ponder how truly grateful we are for our customers, employees, and even our suppliers, we will treat them differently. We will let them know that we "see" them. They are worthy.

Take the time and initiative to learn and acknowledge the names of your employees, regular customers and suppliers. Memorize them along with a few key bits of information about each person. The second time you see a customer and greet him by name and ask how his daughter did at her gymnastics meet, you'll convey to him that he's highly valued—that you're grateful for him.

"People who have good relationships at home are more effective in the marketplace," says Zig Ziglar. Put gratitude into action in your home life, too, and watch the improvement in both your personal relationships and your business productivity. If there are problems at home, you may be more fatigued and stressed, so you won't be able to focus 100 percent at work. Be preemptive. Start a gratitude board both at work and at home. Write brief thank-you notes and post them on the board for all to see. Remember to praise publicly and correct privately.

The happiest people are those who find success in both their careers and their family lives. What good is it to "gain the whole world" through a great business and career only to lose your family? One of the important reasons for having business success is to provide for your family. But if you give your family only money and not you—your heart, mind and time—then they will lack something that money can never buy.

Kerry Egan is a hospice chaplain in Massachusetts and the author of *Fumbling: A Pilgrimage Tale of Love, Grief, and Spiritual Renewal on the Camino de Santiago.* In her work, Egan visits terminally ill people— in their homes, in hospitals, in nursing homes. She tells us, "What people talk about most is their families—their mothers and fathers, their sons and daughters. They talk about the love they felt, and the love they gave. Often they talk about love they didn't receive or the love they didn't know how to offer, the love they withheld, or maybe never felt for the ones they should have loved unconditionally. They talk about how they learned what love is, and what it is not."

The strong probability is that at the end of your life, you won't review what an amazing career you had, how successful your business was, or what kind of house you lived in. You'll either celebrate or lament your relationships with family members and whether you learned to love.

Gratitude is a simple yet effective way to convey importance to another, which is one way to show love to that person. Why not start here and now by thanking your family, friends, co-workers and customers?

Take note of the words of Mother Teresa, that global icon with whom heads of state sought to be seen. "Spread love everywhere you go: First of all in your own house. Let no one ever come to you without leaving better and happier. Be the living expression of God's kindness; kindness in your face, kindness in your eyes, kindness in your smile… There is more hunger for love and appreciation [gratitude] in the world than for bread."

Gratitude allows you to meet this deep-seated need in people, transforming relationships by the sense of kindness it portrays, as well as benefiting you personally in other ways. Being in a state of gratitude changes your body's chemistry and your mind's ability.

Gratitude improves brain function and heart rhythms, thus releasing more good hormones. One of these chemicals is DHEA (dehydroepiandrosterone), which increases vitality and reduces cortisol, the fight-or-flight hormone. In a state of gratitude, you'll be calmer and happier.

Cortisol is also associated with increased belly fat. As you reduce the cortisol in your body, you should be able to shed a few pounds.

The creative process is hindered by cortisol. When your body is in a fight-or-flight mode due to high cortisol levels, your brain is busy scanning your surroundings for danger and escape routes; therefore, your brain cannot be in a creative state. Gratitude reduces the cortisol in your body, thereby freeing your mind to be more creative.

Gratitude is indeed a secret tool. To realize its full benefits, be sure to feel it and express it, not just think it. Apply gratitude liberally and frequently to relationships at work, home and places in between. Then be sure to give yourself an extra heaping dose daily. You deserve it.

Watch as the effects of gratitude fly through the air like a half-court shot—and *swish*—nothing but net.

About Patti

Patti Thor is the founder of Radical Giver. She lives with her family in State College, Pennsylvania. She challenged traditional mindsets in college, corporate America, as an entrepreneur and a full-time mother of four through the principles of Radical Giver.

Her range of experiences helps Patti connect to and challenge the giving heart in all audiences. Patti illustrates secrets to success that encompass the entire being. Health, relationships and spirituality, as well as financial success are integral facets of a fulfilling life. Incorporating Patti's insightful concepts will help you to obtain the whole package.

Patti is a contributing author to *Jump Start Your Success, Volume 2,* featuring Brian Tracy, world-renowned speaker, author and trainer, and James Malinchak, from ABCs hit TV show "Secret Millionaire."

Patti is also author of the upcoming books: *Radical Giver, Radical Giver Tips for Student Leader Success*, and *Radical Giver Secrets to Raising Amazing Kids Without Being a Perfect Parent.*

Patti has a B.S. in Computer Science from the University of Pittsburgh and has received the Insights Foundation Positive Living Strategist Award and Best Speaker Award from the State College Toastmasters. She has spoken at James Malinchak's "College Speaking Success Bootcamp" and Jonathan Sprinkles' "Presentation Power."

To learn more about Radical Giver, visit www.RadicalGiver.com.

CHAPTER 20

Take Aim—and Swing: Reinventing the Golf Coaching Industry

By Peter Hudson

Is there anything more exciting than realizing that a multimillion-dollar turnover industry such as golf coaching is operating in a far-from-results-oriented fashion, and even more incomprehensible that this is something neither the client nor the industry want or seem capable of changing?

The opportunity: How is the World Golf Teaching Federation of Great Britain & Ireland taking advantage of this opportunity, and what new scenarios do we envision in the future?

My company trains people who want to help others play better golf. We believe our philosophies will guarantee their success. We then develop a set of procedures that allow them to deliver results. Once each skill and process is learned, we then give them specific feedback until they can guarantee their client a result every time they teach. The final part of the jigsaw is for them to invest heavily in continual development of their skills in all aspects of the game of golf.

The problem: In the old days, there were no golf shops or online sales—they were located onsite at the golf club—and no standalone driving ranges. A golf course in general had a head professional coach and two to three assistants, depending on the size of the club.

The model had the assistant training to be the head professional coach, and this entailed in 95 percent of cases, the assistant being ensconced in the club. The mathematics of this strategy are obviously flawed unless golf courses tripled in number every three years, which records show is close to being true. What was sad about this strategy was in the beginning the head pro for the most part abused his cheap labor and failed to pass on his coaching skills to his assistant. Unfortunately, this became the norm. How was this allowed to happen—simple, monopoly?

In every other sport, right or wrong, the coaches evolve differently. Sports people play their sport until they lose their competitive edge, then use their experience to pass on their skills by coaching. They may have done this because coaching was the next best thing, or it was their only alternative, but rarely was it because they had always longed to be a coach. The basic golf model was to take young, inexperienced youths and have them teach senior citizens!

A monopoly is great for profit, but is it good for the greater good, or for research and development, or the evolution of coaching? As the age-old saying goes: "If you keep on doing what you have always done, you'll keep on getting what you have always got."

This may explain why golfers don't complain when they have a lesson but don't get better.

Golfers book lessons with expectancy, change coaches with new a expectancy, read articles in golf magazines with new hope, and buy video lessons knowing it offers the ultimate solution, the one thing that will make the most difference. Permanent change for the better, however, is rarely achieved.

How is the World Golf Teaching Federation going about changing this bleak perspective, and what could you learn from our experiences? We've had several issues to understand and discover solutions:

1. How can we change the fundamental flaw in the current system.

2. What would help people to learn what they wanted to learn.

3. What are clients really looking for to achieve from a lesson.

4. What are the criteria for great golf coaching.

5. What process needed to be put in place.

6. What attitudes needed to change both of client and coach.

7. What philosophies needed to be adopted.

8. What additional skills need to be brought into the coaches' curriculum.

9. What limiting beliefs does both client and coach need to become aware of.

10. What supporting beliefs does both client and coach need to adopt.

CHALLENGE 1

We need to build a new model of a perfect coach. Their characteristics may include caring, logical and analytical, passion and enthusiasm, and a sound knowledge of the golf swing, including the basic science and geometry of the swing. They also need an understanding of how to play golf on the course to the highest potential, including preparation, pre-shot routine, course management and state management. Other skills would include communication and people skills.

The lesson model, which accounts for at least 50 percent of the golf improvement business, is based on the idea of one or two short lessons to supply a quick fix. I would put game improvement into three categories:

1. A change in setup that automatically without any need for practice changes the ball flight to what's required—apparent miracle!

2. A change in dynamic movement that requires perfect practice, great feedback and repetition in the playing context (almost impossible for many reasons).

3. A change in expectancy level. Some golfers tend to have high expectations of their performance because at one time they may have holed a 50-foot putt, chipped in, hit greens in regulation with seemingly no effort, and driven the ball miles down the middle of the fairway, and they don't understand why they can't do this every time.

To change this problem, we started recruiting from a more mature demographic, focusing on the skills sets we required rather than relying on the fact that they could play great golf.

CHALLENGE 2

Clients want to get better. If they buy a fridge that says it will maintain the temperature at a certain level, then they'll expect that. If they buy a car that says in urban conditions the car will deliver 38 mpg, they won't be happy if it only delivers 26 mpg.

The client should want a guarantee that they'll reach the agreed-upon target—come on folks that's the least the coach should deliver! The problem is that client doesn't really know what they want and why they want it, and the coach can't deliver.

Now the rest should be straightforward. In our trainings, we started brainstorming what would happen in a first-encounter lesson if the client was paying $750 for a lesson. You can find further details of this on our website: www.becomeagolfcoach.com.

The solution: exceptional customer service before, during and after.

CHALLENGE 3

A coach must love their client and be totally fascinated by their every thought and movement as they think logically and analytically. They must know at least five model swings and the various ways each method has its own variations. They must know the laws of feedback generated by Charles Seashore in his book the *Art of Giving and Receiving Feedback*. The belief that supports this is "no feedback, no learning."

Amazing statistics tell us that just by having a coach we are 50 percent more likely to succeed, and the reason is effective feedback.

The coach needs extensive knowledge of playing golf and an innate desire to improve, no matter their current level. The idea that you have to be a great player has advantages but nowhere near as important as some other skills.

CHALLENGE 4

The processes of learning can be split up into three sections:

1. Lessons
2. Planning
3. Practice

If the average current coach introduced these three elements and took responsibility for each section, there would be a dramatic change in the results most golfers enjoy.

Most coaches act as consultant and tell people what they're doing wrong and what they should do instead. In the information-highway society we live, my mother could tell me what was wrong with my swing and how to correct it. It's in the management of the change where the lesson is lost. What's needed during the practice stage is a nurse, someone to watch closely over the patient.

I was watching a guy on a range; he'd been there four days hitting half-swings, which he instantly reviewed on his video camera. Curiosity got the better of me, and I asked him what he was doing. He said his coach told him not to come back until he could keep the lean on the shaft through impact. He had been given no drill or strategy to achieve this. I asked who was coaching him, and he named one of the country's leading authorities on the golf swing who I know personally and who knows his stuff. This was a lose/lose situation—the client was not going to improve, and the coaches income stream had ended!

The coach's job is to manage the improvement as a project, agree to the goal, make a plan and monitor it, staying flexible throughout until the client's goal is attained.

CHALLENGE 5

The biggest attitude swing required is the coach's ego. Coaches tend to think they're the teacher and reason the client improves and not because they believe in the client and release the genius within them. The only problem is when the client goes to play he is no better. This behavior is compounded by the client who says I hit the ball great when I'm with my coach.

In 2011, I witnessed a plus 2 handicap golfer who was on a coaching course—and had the worst swing I've seen on such a good performer. I found out he had spent time with some of the best coaches in the country, despite which he knew nothing about the golf swing, feedback or anything worthwhile about practice. He was totally reliant on the coach. He had never been encouraged to develop his own intuition and self-worth. The coach needs to help the golfer discover how to improve through awakening and awareness

Coaches who believe in the genius within their client only need to help the client become aware of what they already have. The golf swing is as ancient as time and well ingrained in our DNA. This movement is biomechanical, the same as throwing a stone.

CHALLENGE 6

Philosophies to adopt will include the need to understand and develop powerful feedback skills and three in particular:

1. Information alone won't change a golf swing.

2. Doing something once won't make a habit.

3. Improvement isn't guaranteed until we perform under real life situations.

So much of the industry is based on delivering a massive quantity of information on how to play better, but little is done to manage those changes through great practice. Even more interesting is the coach who rarely watches the golfer play before deciding on how the client can best be helped, which would be far more appropriate place to start.

It's not the information that's important; it's managing the change.

CHALLENGE 7

What additional skills need to be acquired by the golf coach? We're making dramatic inroads, especially in technology. We have full-body motion sensors, high-speed video playback, and force-weight platforms to measure the movements of the center of gravity.

We also have some great work being done by the Titleist institute and Paul Chek in the field of human biomechanics, but this all still falls into the bottomless chasm of information.

Additional skills need to include:

1. Listening (oh yes, we all say we are good listeners!)

2. Questioning

3. Inner game and intrinsic coaching (Tim Galley, Fred Shoemaker)

4. Neurolinguistic and hypnosis

5. Planning

6. Motivational

7. Goal setting

8. Customer service

Without these skills there can be little true rapport, only a vague understanding of the client's goals and no ability to focus on them. The coach won't know when they want them and what any change will bring them. Coaches will have no idea of their commitment and how powerfully motivated they are to achieve their goal.

The power of feedback in learning is not in debate. Feedback can be given externally by the coach, but when the client becomes aware, they can learn so much quicker. These inner game skills will have golfers improving at incredible rates.

Knowing and understanding the power of the unconscious mind in our behavior and learning will massively accelerate the speed at which people can learn anything. This especially true as we discover what beliefs limit and aid our improvement.

Mahatma Ghandi said it best, *"Your beliefs become your thoughts, your thoughts become your words, your words become your actions, your actions become your habits, your habits become your values, your values become your destiny."*

With new information comes a requirement for new skills. What other skills do you think would help coaches be even more effective in realizing the talent we all have within?

CHALLENGE 9

What limiting beliefs do both client and coach need to become aware of; a few we may recognize:

- You can't teach old dogs new tricks.

- I will never be able to play good golf.

- I can teach myself effectively.

- I always miss crunch puts when the pressure come is on.

- I always get nervous on the first tee.

- I don't have any sporting talent.

A few the coach may have:

- Some of my clients will never learn.
- There's no way this person can play scratch golf.
- I know enough.
- I need to know everything, or I can't help.

Change will rarely happen if there's not a supporting belief to drive it. Here are some examples of more positive beliefs we could put in Mr. Ghandi's—and the client's—line diagram:

- I can learn anything I put my energies to.
- I can play to whatever standard of golf I choose.
- Having a great coaching doubles my chances of achieving my goal.
- I always give my crunch puts the best opportunity of going in.
- It is easy to be focused on my goal in any situation.
- I can maximize the talent I have.

Now, for the coach's positive thoughts:

- All of my clients can achieve anything they want.
- Anyone has the potential to play scratch golf.
- I can never stop learning.
- I will always be able to help whatever the challenge.

Every one of these new beliefs will change our behavior for the positive at an unconscious level, putting the coach in much better position to find solutions to the long-standing challenge of changing old habits into new, more resourceful ones.

A successful business stands on three basic premises:

1. A massive demand exists.
2. The demand can be fulfilled.
3. The product/service is successfully marketed.

By listening to golfers (market research) it became obvious that the demand wasn't fulfilled as affectively as the golfers wanted. By finding new and better ways to fulfill the massive demand, all we need to do now is market successfully, and the day-to-day frustrations of playing golf can change into satisfaction, success and happiness, enabling golfers to at last profit from their efforts.

About Peter

Peter is a Level 5 Master Golf Coach, golfing machine Golf Stroke Engineer Master (GSEM), Paul Chek Golf-Bio Mechanic Practitioner with a BSc in sports psychology, a qualified trainer of NLP with SNLP, Reiki Master Practitioner, and registered hypnotherapist.

Peter has been successful in taking a tour player to his first every victory, his county to victory, helped the English amateur team, and assisted thousands of golfers to play better golf. His articles have been published in many of the country's popular golf magazines and featured on many websites, including *Golf Magic*. His main success, however, is the transformation of the coaching industry, how it trains and recruits, and through his philosophy of driving a results-oriented platform.

To learn more about Peter and the WGTF of GB&I, visit www.becomeagolfcoach.com or email info@wgtf.org.uk to discover how you can receive his special report on the *Six Essentials Skills of Earning Money Teaching Golf*. You can also call him on 08450 949445 to find out how you could run your own company training golfers to become golf coaches.

CHAPTER 21

Protect Your Future Wealth! Turbo-Charge Your Brain—It's Your Most Valuable Asset

By Nita Scoggan

Do *you* want to be a millionaire?

When I ask an audience that question there is always a loud response. I've heard them shouting: "Me!" "I do, I do." "Yeah!" or "Me, too, over here!" Most hands are stretched up high. Some people stand and wave their hands, as if I were Santa Claus ready to giveaway big bucks.

I always tell the crowd, "I've got good news for *you*! There's plenty of money for everyone."

After the applause, I caution: "Now for the bad news. Not everyone is going to be a millionaire because of poor health and memory problems. We spend billions on health care, yet Americans have more heart attacks, diabetes and Alzheimer's than even third-world countries. Money can't prevent health or memory problems.

But I have more good news! Are you ready?

If you listen to the cutting-edge information I'm going to share—and act on it—you could be fit and able to earn and enjoy a million dollars. Don't overlook the causes for poor health, even when you're young!

What you discover in these pages will help you find answers to:

1. *What causes health and memory problems*

2. *What you can do to prevent dementia or Alzheimer's*

3. *How you can boost and protect your cognitive abilities*

4. *How to reduce the risk of losing your future wealth and happiness*

5. *Where to find the life changing products you need*

WHAT CAUSES MEMORY AND HEALTH PROBLEMS

A. Stress

Stress is caused by pressure placed on you by the demands of others, such as military training or combat, or the pressures of a new job or demanding boss.

Stress is caused by the demands we place on ourselves, such as striving for all "A's" in college or being a perfectionist.

Stress is caused by grief, anger, jealousy, depression or life situations, such as death of a loved one, divorce, marriage problems, pregnancy, loss of a job, major illness or retirement.

How we handle these affects our physical and mental health.

Why is eliminating stress so important to our health? Because stress can kill. Often heart attacks and strokes can be caused by stress. In the October 2003 *Woman's World* article "Staying Young and Healthy," author Caitlin Castro stated: "Doctors say stress is now our number one health problem and estimates it contributes to as many as 90 percent of all doctor visits."

Stress causes memory loss! When your body is under stress, it produces cortisol as well as adrenalin. The greater the stress, the more cortisol! This disrupts short-term memory. In his book, *The Omega RX Zone*, Dr. Barry Sears states: "…Nothing kills brain cells faster (especially… where memories are stored) than excess cortisol."

B. What you eat can cause memory and health problems.

Many professionals agree healthy eating can lower the risk of Alzheimer's disease. Anne Underwood in the January 19, 2004, *News-*

week article "Now, Reduce Your Risk of Alzheimer's" reported on studies showing there's a correlation. It's wise to cut down or avoid these memory thieves:

- *Refined carbohydrates,* such as potatoes, pasta, bagels, candy, donuts and sugary soft drinks. These make your brain sluggish.

- *Hydrogenated or partially hydrogenated fats* found in cookies, crackers and other bakery goods.

- *Sugar:* Your insulin levels rise with sugar intake. High insulin levels are associated with tumor growth! Excess blood sugar gives the best environment for cancer!

  Dr. Nicholas Perricone states in his book *The Perricone Prescription:* "Sugar reacts with chemicals in our bodies, which is why diabetics age one-third faster than other people when their sugars are poorly managed." And Geoffrey Crowley in the January 2003 Newsweek article states: "Americans have grown sicker and fatter since the USDA Pyramid came out a decade ago."

- *Processed cheese:* Dr. James F. Balch, in the book *Prescription for Nutritional Healing*, warns that processed cheese used in fast-food sandwiches, has a high aluminum content. The addition of aluminum gives the cheese its melting quality, and aluminum is absorbed into your brain, for life!

C. What you drink can cause memory problems.

- *Fluoride:* Dr. William C. Douglas warns of fluoride in tap water: "…in nearly every medically advanced nation, they have banned the practice of fluoridation… Because fluoride makes your body absorb extra aluminum and where does the aluminum go? Your brain!" It's best to try to drink only purified water.

- *Aluminum:* Dr. James F. Balch warns that research found a strong connection between aluminum and Alzheimer's. It's best to avoid aluminum cooking utensils, antiperspirants, drinks in cans, and nonprescription drugs used for inflammation and pain, containing aluminum.

- *Aspartame:* In diet drinks and food, it's recognized as Equal and Nutrasweet, and can cause symptoms that include headaches, dizziness and memory loss. In her book, *The Wisdom of Menopause*, Dr. Christiane Northup says, "Lab studies have proven irreversible brain damage in immature lab animals."

D. Over-the-counter medications can cause memory problems.

- *Diphenhydramine* is found in many over-the-counter medications for sleep, colds and allergies. It decreases acetylcholine levels in the brain. Acetylcholine regulates memory, learning and other cognitive functions. Check the labels; products include: Sominex, Benadryl, Tylenol PM, Excedrin PM and Contact Day and Night.

- *Dextromethoraphan* is found in some cough medicines. This also affects acetylcholine levels in the brain and can impair memory.

Dr. Balch also warns in this book that "pre-senile dementia may strike when an individual is in his 40s."

WHAT YOU CAN DO TO PREVENT PROBLEMS

A. Drink water—it's free! Water wakes up your brain. When your mind gets fuzzy, drink water! Tempted to skip water? Remember, water makes the difference between a grape and a raisin!

Ann Louise Gittleman says in her book *Eat Fat, Lose Weight:* "Water decreases hunger and keeps the brain alert."

B. Avoid dehydration. This can also cause memory problems! Don't wait until you feel thirsty. Tea, coffee, juice, mild or even thin soups help. Dehydration is a major problem among the elderly, resulting in confusion and memory loss.

C. Stop smoking. Dr. James F Balch reported on a study published in the British Medical Journal, *The Lancet,* which stated: *"Smoking more than doubles the risk of developing dementia and Alzheimer's disease."*

D. Exercise—it's free! Get your blood circulating. Growing evidence shows exercise can enhance memory and slow cognitive decline. Fred Gage and the Salk Institute has shown that exercise appears to stimulate the growth of nerve cells in the brain.

Dr. Nicolas Perricone, in the *Perricone Prescription*, says exercise enhances energy, which slows down the effects of aging. It strengthens your heart and boosts oxygen to your brain.

In *What Would Jesus Eat?* Dr. Don Colbert recommends exercising first thing in the morning. Your body has depleted its sugar reserves in the night, so your body will burn fat! More than 90 percent of people know exercise is good, but only 20 percent exercise!

Remember, use it or lose it!

E. Eat for your physical and cognitive health.

1. Eat walnuts, almonds, flax seeds or other nuts—these contain Omega-3, which produce anti-inflammatory substances.

2. Use olive oil for cooking and salads to keep your arteries open.

3. Eat avocados, sardines and pumpkin, which contain Omega-3 fats.

4. Eat unrefined carbohydrates, such as raspberries, blueberries, broccoli, zucchini and green peppers.

5. Dr. Perricone recommends decreasing carbohydrates and increasing protein. Several nutritionals suggest protein at every meal if possible (meat, eggs and fish). He finds that most of us need more Omega-3 (EFAs), which are found in salmon and many cold-water fish. He states: "…fish contains high levels of a substance called DMAE that enhances cognitive function."

6. Dr. Bruce West has been seen by more than 30 million people on national TV. In the Summer 2003 issue of *The Journal of Health Discoveries,* he writes about the alarming percentage of mental and emotional problems caused by the lack of vitamin B complex and Omega-3 in the typical American low-fat diet. He stresses both of these nutrients are crucial for mental health. *"Instead,"* Dr. West explains, *"we load up on Omega-6 fats in vegetable oils…[which] is bad for your health."*

In his book *The Omega RX Zone*, Dr. Barry Spears goes even farther in stating the daily need for Omega-3s: "If you can only do one thing in your life to improve your health, take a daily dose of pharmaceutical-grade fish oil…it has an immediate impact on your eicosanoid levels, and therein lies the key to long-term wellness."

Dr. Sears states that Japanese researchers found students under the stress of exams had an increase in mental alertness after taking a high dose of lecithin prior to their exams! This inexpensive supplement increased their mental recall abilities.

HOW TO BOOST YOUR BRAIN AND AVOID RISK OF FUTURE LOSS OF WEALTH AND HAPPINESS

A. *Take daily vitamins and supplements.* You can't get enough nutrients from the average American diet. You need to read labels on one-a-day vitamins and make sure they contain magnesium, calcium, selenium, B-12 and folic acid. Add alpha lipolic acid, which is proved to help prevent memory loss.

Dr. Perricone recommends alpha lipolic acid. He states it's "400 times stronger than vitamins C and E… it can slow the onset of illness such as Alzheimer's disease, heart disease and arthritis… if you are 40 or older, I suggest you take at least 100 milligrams a day." Dr. Perricone prescribed 50 milligrams of alpha lipolic acid, three times a day, for a patient who complained of memory loss: "It is proven to help prevent the onset of cognitive loss," he says.

B. *Take essential oils (EFAs) supplements.* This includes flax seed oil, fish oils, borage oil, and other oils, such as lecithin and vitamin E. Dr. Sears states that Japanese researchers found that students under stress of exams had an increase in mental alertness after taking a high-dose fish oil supplement, such as lecithin, prior to exams.

The essential oil, phosphatydilserine (fos-fuh-tie-dul-she-reen), known as PS, is found in green vegetables, soy and rice contain. However, the average American only gets a tiny amount or none in their diet. Author Caitlin Castro says, "New research shows getting more PS in supplement form can change our brains for the better." Reporting on the findings of several medical studies, Castro states: "Scientists at the Memory Assessment Clinic in Bethesda, Maryland, report that PS can also improve general learning and memory by 30 percent in three months…"

In *Remarkable Memory Recoveries with PS,* Castro says, "I've had the personal experience with seeing remarkable results in people, in various stages of memory loss, taking PS. One person took 300mg of PS for three months and began noticeable improvement in alertness, energy and memory. Within a year, neurologists where astounded by the remarkable restoration of cognitive function."

Another person no longer recognized her family, couldn't feed or dress herself and spoke almost nothing. Doctors offered no hope, but after taking 500mg for six months she recognized faces and remembered each person's name! She continues to improve, and her dose of PS remains at 300mg a day.

WHERE TO FIND LIFE-CHANGING ITEMS YOU NEED

PS is available at many health-food stores under brand names like Solgar and Source Naturals. Just ask for PS! Or "Neuro PS." Phosphatydilserine is also available at GNC, The Vitamin Shoppes and vitamin stores.

Phosphatydilserine can be ordered from vitamin catalogs, often at a good discount. For example:

• The Vitamin Shoppes: (800) 223-1216
• Swanson's: (800) 437-4148

As always, talk to your doctor before taking any supplement or medication. PS is a soy-based nutrient and has not been found to conflict with any prescriptions.

TURBO-CHARGE YOUR BRAIN

Recognize you must take action. The information I've shared can change your life and save your future wealth. Every 70 seconds someone in America is diagnosed with Alzheimer's! Dr. Gupta on CNN is very concerned because we have an epidemic in America, and "we don't have a cure! And we don't know what causes it!" My research has shown lots of things that cause dementia or Alzheimer's. This information is worth millions. I need to be on Dr. Gupta's program! But there is so much money involved in doctors, prescriptions, nursing homes and nurses.

They don't want you to have this information! Only you can decide to go with diet, vitamins and supplements—and *turbo-charge your brain.* But don't wait. No longer is this disease only for senior citizens—it's striking people in their teens! Go to my website: NitaScoggan.com. There you'll find inspiration and educational articles and testimonials. Miracles are happening! People have recovered from Alzheimer's and others are regaining lost abilities. Invest in Turbo-Charging Your Brain.

About Nita

Nita Scoggan is a national keynote, seminar and international conference speaker. She's the award-winning author of 17 books, professional member of the National Speakers Association, respected adjunct professor and business owner. With enthusiasm and humor she relates success principles learned in her 25-year career as a research analyst and illustrator at the Pentagon. In 2004, Nita was appointed President of the Advisory Board for Oakland City University-Bedford, Indiana. As a member of the OCUB faculty, she teaches business and liberal arts courses. A frequent television guest on national and Canadian programs, Nita stresses the value of education in order to be more successful.

From 1973-1993, Nita gave her lunchtime to God by teaching daily prayer and Bible classes at the Pentagon. Her ministry is credentialed by the Department of Defense Armed Forces Chaplaincy Board. In 1984, Nita was invited to the White House to conduct weekly ministry to the White House staffers. For almost 15 years, from Presidents Reagan to Clinton, teaching focused on prayer, believing in faith and being doers of the Word.

Nita Scoggan is a remarkable woman of faith. Born at her grandmother's home, a 2-pound preemie at birth, the doctor declared she had "no chance to live." But live she did! Placed in a shoebox, fed with an eyedropper—without medical air—her survival was a miracle. She overcame health problems and poverty, giving God the credit for it all. "I believe in miracles! I've seen them, in answer to prayer. I know God can do anything, so I love to pray," says Nita. Her driving force is to uplift, encourage and empower others to achieve their maximum potential in life. Her motto is "Never give up your dreams—pursue them with patience and persistence."

Nita Scoggan
Maximum Zone Consulting
P.O. Box 2125
Bedford, IN 47421-7125
Email: nita.scoggan@gmail.com
www.the-maximum-zone.com

To schedule Nita to speak, call (812) 278-8785.

CHAPTER 22

A Social Network and a Good Product Can Make You Rich!

By Samuel Scott

Direct selling is rapidly gaining popularity today with annual sales of approximately $30 billion in the United States and about $114 billion across the world. As a result of its amazing growth, the direct selling or network marketing industry is often referred to as the business of the 21st century. According to Paul Zane Pilzer, 10 million new millionaires will be created between 2006-2016 and most will come from direct sales and home based business.

This has led to a significant shift toward working for oneself, thus revitalizing conventional ways of making money in the 21st century. What are the main factors in the resurgance of the direct selling industry and why should you want to be a part of it?

BENEFITS OF DIRECT SELLING

First, the lack of job security due to the overall economic downturn has had an adverse impact on employees' job motivation. Admittedly, it can be challenging to maintain motivation to succeed for a company that might fire you tomorrow. Simply put, with direct selling you don't have to worry about firing yourself!

Second, technology is evolving day-to-day; we now live in the world of the internet, which provides access to anything with only a click of the mouse. The world has shrunk with the advent of new technologies, thus making communication easier and quicker. Direct selling is no longer limited to those customers who you can get directly in front of.

Third, every individual wants to take control of their own future, rather than depending on others to decide their future. This can only be possible if you enter into the world of network marketing.

Finally, no where other than direct sales can you get into business for yourself with little or no overhead. This is an ideal startup: The training is free, there are no back-end costs, and you come in via another rep who *wants* you to succeed. In fact, your upline isn't your competition. Your upline wants you to succeed as badly as he wants to succeed himself.

GROWTH IN DIRECT SELLING INDUSTRY

In the past 10 years, the direct selling industry has witnessed tremendous growth. It's the fastest-growing sales channel today, and anyone who takes the risk of entering into this emerging industry will surely attain huge returns. In the year 2009, the number of people who gained success in the field of direct sales exceeded 16 million.

It has been predicted by well-known author and economist, Paul Zane Pilzer that within a decade the number of millionaires in the United States will increase by 10 percent. This figure has more than the double in the last 10 years. And what's more important to us is that most of these millionaires will emerge from the direct sales industry.

What lies behind this prediction is the fact that this industry offers a chance to earn extremely high incomes provided that you take the opportunity seriously. You might be surprised to know that you can earn up to $100,000 or more per month through direct sales…with *no* overhead!

MISCONCEPTIONS: WHO CAN BENEFIT FROM DIRECT SALES?

Despite the enormous gains associated with direct selling, only 1 percent of the world's population is involved in direct selling, due to misconceptions. (Therefore, 99 percent of the *world* is your potential customers). Many people have the opinion that it works on a pyramid scheme, which means not everyone can be successful and only a few fortunate people receive profits. Others believe that they might end up being unable to sell their products and services through direct selling.

However, all these perceptions are far from reality, since many people fail to understand the basic idea behind the direct selling industry. The low profile of this industry is the underlying reason for the lack of understanding.

The truth is that anyone can succeed in direct selling if they have three simple qualities: a passion for the product, a desire to succeed, and the ability to be coachable. Some of the most successful people in direct sales are people who come from humble beginnings. In this industry, it's not the letters behind your name that determines your success, it's your burning desire to succeed and adherence to the system the company has in place.

EXPERT OPINIONS ON DIRECT SELLING

Nevertheless, direct selling is known to be the best kept secret in the world. Many financial experts are of the view that direct selling is a "recession-proof" industry. Among the most successful investors in the world is Warren Buffett, who says, "Direct sales is the best investment I've ever made."

Bill Gates stated, "If I were given a chance to start all over again, I would choose network marketing." Robert Kyosaki calls it "The business of the 21st century." So those of you that still think that this exploding lucrative business model is a sham...think again.

6 STEPS TO DIRECT SALES SUCCESS

1. Find a Company With Simple, Proven, Duplicateable System
Look for a product you can get passionate about and has a duplicateable system that doesn't require you to jump through hoops. You want a simple system that's easy for you and other potential business partners to understand. The system should be a three-step process: expose, educate, signup. You want a direct selling opportunity that gets you face to face and relationship building as quickly as possible. If it's too hard for you to understand or duplicate, you won't be successful.

If you look at the most successful direct selling opportunities in the world, the ones with longevity like Amway, Mary Kay, Avon to name a few, you'll find a simple and straightforward success plan that so basic a child can do it.

2. Mind-set: The Foundation of Success In Any Endeavor

Everyone has a "why" story. What's yours? Writing out your "why" story will keep you motivated throughout your sales journey. It's said that your "why" should make you cry.What does that mean? It means that your reason(s) for succeeding in this business are so strong that they move you, and others, to tears and to *action...massive action.*

Keeping the correct mind-set will keep you driven to succeed. It will keep you focused on the prize when faced with rejection. Understand and accept the fact that many people will say "no." It isn't personal. They're simply saying no to the opportunity. Many will follow once they see your success; just keep exposing people to the life-changing opportunity. Remember your "why," and then see yourself already successful. See yourself relaxing on the beaches of the world, while your check continues to hit your mailbox week after week, driving your dream vehicle, and living in your dream home. See your kids in the best college with no financial concern...this is what we call lifestyle.

3. Accountability: Have a Goal

Set out on a mission to change people's lives, including your own. Set your financial goals and think only of getting to the next promotional level. Whether or not you're looking to earn an extra $500 a month or $50,000 a month, it must be in writing. If your plan isn't on paper, you don't own it. Write down your daily game plan, how many people you're going to talk to and where you want to be in 30, 60, 90 days. Move ahead one position at a time in your company. Direct sales is the only business where you can promote yourself to the next position and earn unlimited amounts of income, but it all starts with a plan of action. During my eight years in network marketing, my goal in each company I joined was to create a success story. I accomplished this by breaking records in the first 30 days so I could position myself with the company, and business partners, as a leader. People follow leaders and buy into the opportunity because they believe in you, not because of the product.

Remember the ultimate goal is to build residual income so you can enjoy maximum time freedom. Map out your short- and long-term goals, three to five years, create a plan of action, execute your plan and then sit back and live off the fruits of your labor.

4. Receptive: Be Coachable

Listen to the successful people in your upline—those who have recently been where you are as you begin your business. There's no need to reinvent the wheel. If your upline recommends a strategy that works, use it!

Sometimes coming from a corporate background—which is substantially more structured than direct selling—can be a drawback. Quite often, the most successful people who enter the direct sales arena are people who have no experience or are simply new to the industry.

5. Team: Build an Army

Share the opportunity with everyone. I like to use the analogy that building your team is like flipping cards in a deck. Your goal is to locate the aces, leaders that have the same hunger for success that you have. Then just keep flipping the cards, sifting and sorting, until you find at least five aces. Now all you have to do is teach them how to do the exact same thing and before you know it, you will have thousands of business partners all over the world. The exponential growth potential of direct sales is the engine that drive this wealth building machine.

Some direct sales businesses, like Evolv Health, which is one of the businesses I've recently started, make it fairly easy to build your team because of their customer health challenge concept. For example, instead of trying to fight for the 1 to 5 percent of the population that's doing network marketing, their focus is on getting customers on a health challenge. By getting people to take an 84-day health challenge—and allowing them to get their products for free, by getting three of their friend to take the challenge with them—they have put in place a very simple duplicateable success system that literally grows on its own. There's no mention of network marketing during the in-home challenge parties. However, those that are interested in becoming a promoter will meet at a different time. Now that's how you build an army…give people what they want.

6. Replicate the Process

Once you have your team in place, replicate the process. In 36 to 72 months you can earn more monthly than a doctor or a lawyer earns in a year. Keep to the system. All too often people fail in direct sales because they get bored with or sloppy about the process. Get out of your own way! You've heard "If it ain't broke, don't fix it." Why would you change or deviate from a system that's working for you?

PROMOTE YOURSELF *AND* GIVE YOURSELF A RAISE *NOW*

Why wait on your day job to give you a 3 percent raise at the end of the year? Even if you only began your direct selling career with the goal of paying off one bill per month, it would likely be worth more to you than your 3 percent raise. If you learned nothing else from this chapter, give yourself a raise by maximizing your profitability by exchanging hours of hard work for hours of *smarter, leveraged* work.

About Samuel

Samuel Scott is a life-enhancement coach and uses network marketing and martial arts as his vehicles for personal development. He is the founder and CEO of Full Circle Martial Arts Academy in Glenn Dale, Maryland. At age 37, Samuel fired the government to pursue his dream of changing people's lives and teaching them how to do the same.

As a network marketer, in 1996 Samuel was one of four leaders selected by a telecommunications company to launch local phone services on the East Coast. He was able to help thousands of people earn a substantial income and pursue their life dreams. Since then, Samuel has ventured in to different companies, including legal services, where he became a Director in 57 days; a video technology company, where he achieved Presidents Club status and won a S550 Mercedes; and now a health and wellness company, which he feels will be his most fulfilling venture. He has committed to helping his new company, Evolv Health, put 8.4 million people thru an 84-day health challenge over the next 10 years.

Samuel believes that serving others is the secret to becoming wealthy beyond your wildest dreams.

CHAPTER 23

The Swaggitude of Success: Harness Your "It Factor" for the Long Term

By Sonja Landis

There's an undeniable "It Factor" of success...a swagger, an attitude, an energy that can't be mistaken. You know when a person walks in the room and people can't help but notice? (And not in the bad way, as in toilet-paper-stuck-to-their-shoe kind of notice!)

While some people certainly have a natural abundance of that "swaggitude," it's something anyone can cultivate, grow and exude in their daily life. Everyone started somewhere, even the swaggiest of moguls!

An integral part of swaggitude derives from interest. Jim Rohn says there are only two things you need to build interest in, and you'll quickly and exponentially increase your It Factor for success: life and people. You build interest in life by taking an active role, engaging your senses, and actually moving your *chi* (which is like a**, but not a cuss word) instead of watching other people's lives on E! and Bravo. You develop your interest in people by actually listening to conversations, thoughtfully asking productive questions, and not trailing off into those deep thoughts of what Snooki did last night on "Jersey Shore" (ohnoshediiii-ennnt!). Your ultimate and long-term success depends on high levels of interest, both in you and also from you.

Interesting, caring people with genuinely interesting life experiences spark enthusiasm and a larger-than-life personality that draws audiences in. They've seen more things with their own eyes, whether it be the Egyptian pyramids or a butterfly hatching out of a cocoon on a simple nature hike. They have interesting things to talk about, and the topics don't concern any of the "Housewives." Besides being interesting, a person with the "swaggitude of success" has an essence, bigger than brains, looks, or talent, that makes him/her stand apart from the rest, projecting a positive energy that radiates beyond them, explaining that mesmerizing magnetism! It, quite simply, feels good to be around them! So you're saying, *alright Sonja, I'm down. Tell me what and how to increase my swaggitude. Define what you're talkin' 'bout, sister! And I say, with pleasure, my new friend!*

SWAGGITUDE OF SUCCESS TRAIT #1: SPELLBINDING CHARISMA 2.0

Charisma is one of those difficult-to-describe-but-easily-detected anomalies of the human race. It combines enthusiasm and interest in people and life, which we discussed before, with the ability to connect and establish common bonds with others, and inspire devotion in them. *Psychology Today* refers to this as "synchrony," stating that if two people click, they unconsciously adjust their posture, facial expressions, and speech rate to match each other. Charismatic people tend to be the leader of this synchronization. The way this element becomes Spellbinding Charisma 2.0 is by taking it to the next level, which is *Charismatic Communication. That's* what's gonna set you apart, folks. A charismatic communicator speaks with personality and life experiences to connect with their audience, imagery to inspire devotion and deepen emotional ties, and the overlapping components of sensitivity, control, confidence and genuine expression. It doesn't mean you're the best, most perfectly trained, velvety-smooth-voice-over-quality communicator. It means instead you're a bonding agent, rich in metaphors, interest, care and connection with your audience, and it means that you communicate uniquely, with your own style. No one will be just like you, and you won't be just like anyone else. Embrace the individuality you bring to the world, be aware and consciously practice charismatic communication in your own way, and then get yourself out there to make a positive impact on people, whether you communicate in the written or spoken word.

- *Sensitivity:* Respect for your audience, keeping in mind some of their values, beliefs, and pleasure/pain triggers. Sensitivity also includes an ability to make adjustments based on those things, even on the fly.

- *Control:* The pitch, tone, pace and clarity of your communication, all of which can apply either in written or spoken form.

- *Confidence:* You can increase your self-confidence in communication by concentrating on the message you deliver, the benefit you provide to others, instead of being self-absorbed by personal insecurities. This comes with practice, wisdom and grace, which we'll talk more about soon! You can hardly wait?!?! I know! Me, too!

- *Genuine Expression:* Stop trying so hard, and just be natural. If you're speaking, take your hands out of your pockets, unfold your arms, and let them hang down. Not like an ape, but just unrestrained. Now talk. Your gestures and facial expressions will naturally and genuinely add to your communication within a minute or two, and you don't have to plan them out or spend any energy thinking about them!

- *Optional:* Humor: Let's be frank here…most people like comedy. Most people, with a soul and a reflection, like to laugh because it feels good! It immediately connects and synchronizes people, eases tension and nervousness, and actually releases endorphins in the brain that can open up creativity and problem-solving pathways. Laughter also gives an instant energy surge in the body, like one of those Listerine strips, but without the Listerine strip. I'm a big believer in the use of humor, and although my study is unofficial at this point, I would say that approximately 98.3 percent of the population would consider the use of a little humor part of charisma and charismatic communication.

Charisma and Charismatic Communication are based, at least partially, on the image you project with your looks and communication. They include your first impression, dress, hairstyle, posture, walk, body language and appearance, which are all important but also somewhat surface level. An image. Translation: You need to bring more to the table than just your Spellbinding Charisma 2.0, toots, so let's move on.

SWAGGITUDE SUCCESS TRAIT #2:
PASSIONATE, COURAGEOUS CONFIDENCE

Straight up: You gotta have a pair. Really. You've got to have some nerve, and take some risks. You've got to not just "be willing" to fail but actually do it, and do it hard. I mean the floundering and seriously-hurt-feelings kind of fail. Why? Because the biggest failures lead to success, blah blah blah, and also because being embarrassed by or afraid of failure is your ego, flexing on ya. Without colossal failure under your belt, you'll never be fully in charge…your ego will.

Ego had an important job historically: to protect your pretty, little self. The ego sets off internal danger signals, which served an awesome purpose when we were hunting/being hunted by saber-toothed tigers in our loin cloths. Now, however, your ego is wrapped up in what *society* dictates as good or bad, and it can hold you back from great achievement. Failing, falling flat on your sweet face, is the best way to start to get that ego in check. Once you try things, they don't work out, and you wake up again to live another day, you'll start to be in control of the ego. You can and should make friends with your ego, too! Tell him/her that you understand his/her role for protection but that you're going to also try new things that feel uncomfortable at first, that it's part of developing your swaggitude of success!

Acknowledging the possibility of failure, even being prepared to appreciate it when it happens, thanks to your newfound ego-knowledge, allows a person to be nervy and take chances. Big ideas, and big achievements for our planet, weren't always immediately embraced, so be ready! You can't let that fact derail you with your enthusiasm. You've got to be excited about what you're doing…passionate! See your work, career, business and life as the adventure that they really are! Success and failure are both part of it, so go ahead! Jump in and get excited for the ride! Now I'm no superhuman, but I know you were totally thinking that I am, and I know it's hard to be as passionately excited about failure as you are about success. I get it. You have to, if nothing else, view the failures as opportunities for adjustments, moving forward with your next steps, getting you closer to the success you crave. Sometimes the world is not quite ready for extreme fabulousness, but having the courage to put new ideas and your unique talents out there as a contribution to others will serve you well. Anyone with swagger, success, and courage started somewhere, just like you and me. I now give you permission to be more courageous. Go ahead and give permission to yourself, and watch the magic happen! After you fail, of course. Most likely, the magic comes after some epic fails. Just sayin'.

Darren Hardy, publisher and CEO of *Success Magazine*, has a great pendulum analogy with success/failure: The greater it swings to one side, the greater it swings to the other. If you stay still, you never really fail or get a lot in return. Your ego is *really* in control here! If you fail just a little, fall prey to the panic of your ego, and swing just a little in the success realm, you'll stay right there, back and forth in your comfort zone. Let me tell you a secret to life: The magic happens outside your comfort zone! If you get that ego in check, swing big, accept and acknowledge big failure, you'll be ready to swing big on the success side, too!

Ok, so where are we...courageous? Check. Now let's talk confidence and the different aspects that entails. There's self-confidence: the belief in *your own* ability, skills, and knowledge to perform a task or activity with the probability of achievement; and then there's a confidence you can develop in others: the belief in another person, or team of people, to work together with combined abilities, skills, and knowledge to achieve and perform effectively and successfully. Both play important roles in your swaggitude because the former without the latter gives off a selfish, self-indulgent, arrogance that will directly erode the charisma and connections you establish. The last and very important aspect of confidence is in a higher meaning, God, Source, fate, the Universe, or whatever label you feel comfortable using here. A person with swagger, success, and that "It Factor" has a calm confidence that things—challenges, setbacks, failures, and fears—are all part of the road to inevitable success. This peaceful belief allows them to start their path, move forward, fail, renegotiate their relationship with the ego, and confidently pursue their own unique success. You have to trust. You. Have. To. Trust! In something!

SWAGGITUDE OF SUCCESS TRAIT #3:
GRACE UNDER FIRE, FIERCE YET BENEVOLENT WISDOM

Awww yeah, fancy pants! We're talking classy, genuine charm and kindness now! Here is where a connection with people and the ability to charismatically communicate combine with the calm confidence of a higher power, producing something truly beautiful: poise. Poise (or grace) moves past the mere (yet important!) image of charisma into the undeniable truth of it. This is where a person will prove their power and swagger are for the greater good, instead of only self-serving or crazy-purple-kool-aid-drinking ways. Evil people have had charisma; they've *lacked* grace, benevolence, wisdom and insight. People who embody these characteristics are still fierce in their pursuits of success, just as passionate as any others at the top, but they also provide wise and positive meaning in their pursuit. They add value to the life experience, for themselves as well as others.

People who possess Swaggitude Trait #3 radiate a sense of humility and gratitude. They have tremendous swag, yet equally understand we all enter this world the same basic way: crying, exposed, and wondering what the holy halibut is going on. There isn't an elitist attitude, in spite of great successes in business or in life. They have great sensitivity and can connect with others in a way that inspires and bonds, rather than boasts and gloats. I believe the technical term for the latter is arrogant jerk, but I could be mistaken. Don't quote me on that one…

- *Grace:* Practicing conscious control over personal feelings of discomfort, poise in conflict, and respectful communication skills toward an elevated, positive agenda or compromise. A person with grace maintains a calm and composed demeanor, even when things get messy and life presents its ups and downs.

- *Benevolance:* Kindness and compassion for the greater good of people, animals, or the planet.

- *Wisdom:* To provide meaning, life-experiences, and introspective knowledge for the purpose of moving through problems or incidences quickly. A study at the University of California, Berkeley shows that while a young person can demonstrate wisdom, it increases between the ages of 27 and 52. (http://www.psychologytoday.com/articles/200505/the-x-factors-success)

- *Insight:* Providing peaceful perspective and a deeper meaning to the experiences, situations, life lessons and characteristics of swaggitude, and using them all for positivity and success!

The fact that you read this chapter, the simple awareness of these swagger elements, will plant a couple seeds of knowledge on your journey in life. That alone will grow your swagger factor exponentially. You already know more and are further along the path of success than the majority of people in the world, simply by reading this chapter. High five!

Cultivating your "It Factor" and swaggitude of success is an ongoing and enjoyable process that will serve you throughout your lifetime. It's a necessary component in the foundation of You Inc., but it's only half the equation to increase your revenues, income and impact. The next part is to strategically implement a solid marketing campaign, using all those elements of swagger you've worked on, to impact your target market of clients and serve them well.

To make real money and fill your bank account with cashola instead of love, intentions and affirmations, you need to make yourself, your products or services, *available* and *valuable* to others. This is where we truly implement a strategy that showcases you, your swagger, your "It Factor" in the marketplace. It includes unique branding, marketing, copywriting, logo, professional images, website, mission statement, target market, products, and services, all of which embodies and communicates the swaggitude you've developed and grown! You're positioned as an expert and authority in your field, and you've got the ethical characteristics in line to back it up.

This part of the equation can (and should!) include press releases, media, article and video marketing, online/offline/mobile marketing campaigns, integrity and personality. It can (and should!) emulate other successful people who've gone before you, yet have the distinction and voice that's all you.

None of this is a quick and dirty, cheap and easy, one-stop-shop scheme to success. This is an investment in your long-term amazingness and impact on the world, which will directly reflect in your bank account when done properly. I can't promise you it will be easy, but I can promise you that *you don't have to do it alone,* and that it's all worth it, not just in the end, but along the way, too!

About Sonja

Custom Develop the "It Factor" for Long-Term Career & Lifestyle Success

Author, Artist, Speaker, Entertainer, Entrepreneur, Mom. Self-Proclaimed Comedienne. Self-Proclaimed Superhero. Teller of Stories, Laugher of Jokes, Lover of Carbs, Loser of Keys.

Sonja is a popular author, speaker, guest contributor, media personality, and marketing expert who's regularly sought out for her entertaining and insightful opinions and strategic tips on career progression, business development and marketing campaigns that *really work*. She delivers a relevant, timely, empowering message, inspiring people to live and contribute uniquely on their very own cutting edge, combining soul-stirring wisdom with sharp business, career, life and marketing advice.

She's the Artist/Owner of The Painted Laugh Studio & Art Gallery in Southern California, where she custom-paints *laughter* for numerous celebrity clients…and she's the only one in the world who does! She's been featured on Fox, NBC, and *OK!* magazine, among others.

Sonja travels the country speaking to college and university students, entrepreneurs and small-business owners, helping them flex and transform marketing, branding, and media/PR skills for the future.

Applauded for her charisma, energy and engaging humor throughout her work, Sonja connects with her audience like an old friend. She's a new kind of role model and a dynamic spokesperson for many generations, bridging the gap between X, Y and the Millennials. Her concrete strategies increase bottom-line revenues, skyrocket confidence and "swaggitude," and ignite the most necessary aspects of success: *living* fully engaged, being *inspired* by what you do, *loving* who you are, and *contributing* to the good of our planet.

She's author of *My Master's Degree Is Useless?!?!* for adults (incredibly funny and inspirational, but rated R for language), *Think Different! The Illustrated Story and Life Lessons of Steve Jobs* for readers age 6 plus, and the upcoming kids' series *The Big Book of Bios: Important Values, Characteristics, and Attitudes of Success From Modern Day Role Models* (the factual biography, timeline, famous quote(s) and illustrations of 21 modern-day role models for readers age 6 plus).

Sonja lives in San Diego, California, with her son, two idiot dogs (whom she adores), and a newly obtained spotted-leopard gecko (whom she thinks is alright). As if that weren't enough, her boyfriend just adopted a hunk o' ridiculousness from San Diego Bulldog Rescue. He's pretty much the cutest thing ever. The dog. But for the record, her boyfriend is no slouch, either.

To learn more about Sonja Landis, "The Swaggitude of Success," and receive FREE, simple, success-driven marketing elements you can apply to all aspects of your life and career *right away*, visit www.MeetSonja.com. She accepts a *very limited* number of private clients and completely implements a full campaign for them, dramatically increasing traffic, sales conversion and revenue…for about the cost of hiring a receptionist to answer the phones for a month. The *right information* and p*ersonalized style* is what you need to make the difference you're here to make…*Mission: united in the journey, unique in the implementation.*

CHAPTER 24

Top 10 Steps to Achieve Greater Success, Overcome Adversity and Win the Game of Life

By John R. Salkowski

I'm John R. Salkowski and this is my success story…

"Develop success from failures. Discouragement and failure are two of the surest stepping stones to success."—Dale Carnegie

I can remember way back into my childhood that nothing ever came easy to me. I wasn't a gifted child. I wasn't blessed with God-given talent. Everything I did or wanted to do was always a challenge. It was always an uphill battle for me. I say that not for pity but because it's the truth. At a very young age I can remember someone saying, "What doesn't kill you makes you stronger." I believe that today. I also believe you get out what you put in. Facing adversity was part of my life and has created the person I am today.

ADVERSITY BREEDS SUCCESS

"Adversity causes some men to break; others to break records."
—William Arthur Ward

Adversity has shaped me into the person I am today. I am who I am today because of the lessons and challenges I have confronted in my life. Everything I am today was self-taught. I had no father figure, mentor or role model in the early stages of my life. The most important time in a human being's life is adolescence. During this time is when your mind and body is shaped and sculpted. No one taught me how to succeed. No one taught me how to be a winner in life. If I wanted to succeed I had to teach myself. I could have felt sorry for myself because of the deck of cards I was dealt. Instead, I accepted that hand of cards and made something out of it. There were no excuses for me. I don't believe in excuses. I only knew adversity in my life. If I wanted to break through the adversity I had to out-work everyone else. That is just what I did. Below are steps I've followed to overcome my adversity:

TOP 10 STEPS TO ACHIEVE GREATER SUCCESS, OVERCOME ADVERSITY AND WIN THE GAME OF LIFE

1. *Talk to someone you can trust in the field.* Explain how important this goal is to you. Explain how you're feeling. Ask for their advice if they were faced with X. I didn't have this. You *need* to do this before you give up.

2. *Ask your family and friend(s) who know you for their opinions.* Stay away from the Nay-Sayers, Negative Nellies and Jealous Jackie's.

3. *Take a step back.* Take the time you need to think about the consequences if you stop pursuing your goal/dream. What will the outcome be if I stick with this? What will the outcome be if I walk away?

4. *Practice positive talk.* I can do this! I can make it! I am important! I am a great person! I am successful!

5. *Learn everything you possibly can.* Seek out someone who has accomplished what you want to accomplish. Take them out to lunch and learn from them.

6. *Commit to goals, short term and long term.* Start with the end in mind—long-term goal—and work backward when writing goals.

7. *Work on your dream every day of your life.* Fill all the minutes and hours you've allotted with serious determination one day at a time.

8. *Give it all you can.* There will be days when you don't feel like giving it your best. Give it your best anyway for that day.

Do not cheat yourself by not pursuing your dream. Give it everything you've got. If you have to walk away, know that you gave it your all. Live with no regrets!

9. *Keep a journal.* Write down what you accomplish every day. Just a few words will do, or else you'll create yet another job, which you don't need.

10. *Celebrate your achievements!* Reward yourself with predetermined gifts. Treat yourself. For your ultimate goals, give yourself the greatest reward, then set new goals. You can achieve more!

CREATING MY OWN DESTINY

"It is not in the stars to hold our destiny but in us."
—William Shakespeare

I had no one to count on when things got tough. I had no one to turn to when I needed advice. The only person I could count on was the man in the mirror. I knew that I couldn't do it alone.

If I wanted to be truly successful in life, I had to model and study successful people. This is exactly what I did.

At the time in my life, I was working as a police officer in a very prominent and affluent community. I would drive around looking at these multimillion-dollar mansions, wondering to myself, What is it that these people do to make so much money.

While on patrol one day, I received a radio call to check a residential alarm. What you're about to read changed my life forever.

As I pulled up to the residence, I immediately was in awe. The house was beautiful. It was a multimillion-dollar mansion. I said to myself, This will be me one day.

I walked up to the front door and was greeted by the homeowner; we'll call him John Doe for anonymity reasons. I introduced myself and followed through with my business. After I was through, I had a conversation with this gentleman that was amazing.

As we began to talk, I happened to ask him what he did for a living. He told me he owned his own company. I, of course, asked him what kind of business, and he told me commercial real estate. As we continued our conversation, he told me that he only has a high school education. He did tell me that he believes in secondary education, but it wasn't in the cards for him. He credits his humble and poor beginnings to creating his hunger for success and becoming a self-made multimillionaire who came from a poor section of Philadelphia. I asked him what qualities he possessed that he credited to his success. He told me determination, perseverance and self-discipline.

I told him a little about me and what I had overcome. The last question I asked John changed my life forever. I asked him if he could give me any advice on success, what it would be. He told me to read the book, *Rich Dad, Poor Dad* by Robert Kiyoski.

The first thing I did when I got home was order that book. I read it in one day.

I believe we are put on this earth for a reason. We are put in certain places for a reason. We meet certain people for a reason. I believe I was meant to meet this man on this very day who I give a lot of credit to for my success. The conversation I had with him was priceless, and I will always be so grateful for his time.

From this point on, my mindset, my outlook, my attitude changed, and so did my success.

SUCCESS LEAVES CLUES

"Mentoring is a brain to pick, an ear to listen, and a push in the right direction."—John C. Crosby

I knew if I wanted to be successful, I would have to find someone I could follow and model. I wanted to find someone I admired, trusted and respected. I also was looking for someone who started from humble beginnings as I did. Someone who had the rough road I did, but now is living a self-made life.

I began doing some research on people who grew up poor but have turned themselves into self-made people. Self-made, meaning coming from nothing and building an empire of fortune and success. I came across Napoleon Hill and Brian Tracy. I was so intrigued by their successes, I began to study them like a surgeon performing brain surgery.

Napoleon Hill

> *"Plans are inert and useless without sufficient power to*
> *translate them into action."*—Napoleon Hill

Napoleon Hill was born into poverty in 1883 in a small one-room cabin in Virginia. He began his writing career as a journalist for a small-town newspaper and worked his way through law school. He became a respected attorney and a bestselling motivational writer.

Many thousands credit Napoleon Hill's book *Think and Grow Rich* as the beginning foundation of their financial and personal success. Hill passed away in November 1970 after a long and successful career writing, teaching and lecturing about the principles of success. His work stands as a monument to individual achievement and is a cornerstone of modern motivation.

Millions of people continue to learn from his life-changing books and audio programs.

Brian Tracy

> *"More people are becoming more successful at a faster rate than any*
> *other time in history. There have never more opportunities to turn your*
> *dreams into reality than there are right now."*—Brian Tracy

Brian Tracy is one of America's leading authorities on the enhancement of personal effectiveness, the development of human potential and the art of salesmanship. A dynamic speaker, he has motivated and inspired thousands of people toward peak performance and high achievement. His seminars on leadership, goals, motivation, time management and success psychology draw capacity audiences.

I began implementing what I've studied from Napoleon Hill and Brian Tracy into my life. My life was starting to change for the better. What I began doing that changed my life is below. If you implement these strategies, stay focused and disciplined, your life will change, too.

TOP 10 LAWS TO ACHIEVE SUCCESS
AND WIN THE GAME OF LIFE

1. *Be Decisive in all you do.* The decisions you make will define your destiny.

2. *Stay laser focused.* By focusing on something you want or want to achieve, it becomes like a magnet that pulls you and the resources you need to achieve them.

3. *Set goals.* This is a *must:* Write down all the goals you want to achieve each night before going to sleep. The goals must specific, measurable and time bounded.

4. *Make a plan.* Without a plan you will wander like a boat without a rudder.

5. *Surround yourself with positive, successful, influential people.* Follow their lead and *do not* reinvent the wheel.

6. *Encourage failure.* Failure is a *must* if you want to succeed. Embrace it and learn from it.

7. *Take action.* Do what is necessary each and every day to get you closer to your prize. Without action, you'll remain in the same spot.

8. *Inspect what you expect.* Your attention toward your goals will increase productivity.

9. *Reward yourself.* You *must* reward yourself once you accomplish your goal—positive reinforcement.

10. *Practice commitment and perseverance.* Commit yourself, hold yourself accountable, and stay focused on your mission.

About John

John R. Salkowski is a retired police officer after an impressive 15-year career. He's also a survivor of PTSD (Post Traumatic Stress Disorder) from a shooting incident that eventually ended his career. John has been diagnosed with this illness since 2000. He has received numerous Distinguished Awards for Bravery, Merit and Unit Citations. He has also received several employee recognition awards for his work within the community.

After his police career, John got into real estate sales and entrepreneurship. John's approach to business is dedicating himself to helping others succeed. John founded his own company, JRSRealtyGroup.com, in 2008. He has built a reputation as a motivated professional with unwavering integrity and honesty. As one of the top realtors in the country, John contributes a lot of his success to offering both buyers and sellers watertight guarantees. John has been featured in *Philadelphia* magazine as the area's top real estate expert several years in a row.

John's true passion is speaking. The topics he covers are on leadership, inspiration, motivation, success, overcoming adversity and finding your why power. John speaks to business organizations, colleges, high schools and youth groups. In 2010, John founded AchieveSuccessAcademy.com where he shares his passion in helping others find theirs. He is also an avid blogger. John is currently working on two other books on leadership success that will soon be published.

In his free time, John enjoys exercising, reading, writing, blogging, traveling, and spending time on the beach with his daughter, Alexa.

CHAPTER 25

The HE*ART* of Business Communications: How Every Interaction Affects the Bottom Line

By J.L. Ashmore

Early in my training and consulting career, there was a large corporation that was interested in improving their customer relations by educating their front-line employees in ways to deal with clients more effectively. I was a contract consultant with a training company at the time and taught a communication skills program that gave the front-line of any organization the skills to respond to customers in ways that left them with a positive perception of the service provider—the HE*ART* of the business communication.

I'd been teaching this program in the government, telecommunications, financial and service industries for 10 years by that time, so my skills were well honed in this area. On this occasion, however, I was on the tail end of traveling and training clients in various time zones across North America for seven weeks in a row. As one might imagine, I'd stretched myself physically and emotionally to a place of considerably less tolerance of the daily stresses of this kind of work relative to what I had trained myself to normally tolerate as a traveling consultant facilitating three- to five-day classes.

It was fulfilling to me that throughout my client base and my group of colleagues, at the time, I was known for very effectively modeling the skills I was teaching and even received rewards and recognition for doing so. How credible is it after all for a consultant or any teacher, for that matter, to not practice what they preach? So I had cultivated a discipline of practicing the principles I sincerely believed in and taught.

At the last of my seven weeks of travel, however, I encountered a loss of the energy required to maintain that discipline. While facilitating at this particular company at the end of my stretch, I encountered a participant with some behaviors that caught me off guard. This was someone I observed interacting before class and after breaks with her fellow employees in a way that demonstrated arrogance, manipulation and a general lack of kindness. Regretfully, my mind was way too quick to judge in that moment, and I was not at all in touch with any sense of compassion in my heart.

In a rested and clear state of mind, I would normally have been able to respond to such a person in a way that wouldn't reveal any internal personal reaction I might have to such behavior. I might have rationalized in my mind a favorite mantra from one of my teachers: "We all do the best we can with the resources we have." I could also have connected with her on a more human, heartfelt level, and attempted to learn/ understand more about her. I truly didn't know if she might have just lost a loved one, been dealing with a health challenge, or been abused as a child. There was no sense of compassion coming from me!

Unfortunately, on this occasion, as the saying goes, I tripped and fell on my own sword. After she had made a comment in class, the content of which is irrelevant but which did carry a tone of arrogance, a feeling of judgment and intolerance arose in me that provoked an inappropriate word to escape from my mouth, partially in reaction to her comment in class and mostly reacting to what I had observed and judged regarding her behavior with her co-workers. Not good on my part! Rather than positively acknowledge in a neutral tone of voice, what she, my customer, had said, my acknowledgment began with the reactionary word "Obviously…" I believe the entire sentence that came out of me was something like, "Obviously, that would be the case."

At that time, the course I was teaching had a list of effective and ineffective words to use in a customer situation. Although the word "obviously" wasn't on that list, it tends to be a word quite commonly heard from the lips of salespeople who are interacting with potential clients. Examples might be: "Obviously you can see how this works" or "Obviously you can see how you need this product." I now teach and coach salespeople and recommend they become conscious of using the word "obviously." They quickly see that the use of the word is synonymous with saying, "As any fool can see…" It's discounting and comes from the judgmental mind versus the compassionate heart.

On that fate-filled day, I was teaching the communications program, that word "obviously" landed on the participant in the workshop as if I had most adamantly said, "As any fool can see…" She was upset and at the break went to her manager to complain about the rude and obnoxious person teaching her class, that the workshop and I were a farce and should be cancelled and not allowed to be taught in their company again! You might think that was a strong reaction on her part, but she could have been related to the owner of the company and had an arm of power unbeknownst to me. In that moment, for all I knew, not only did I stand to lose my contract with the training company, but the training company was at risk of losing the $200,000 contract with the client.

Fortunately, the manager came to me to discuss the situation. Not only did I acknowledge and apologize for my error to the manager but I did so directly to the participant. Plus, in making up for the error, I gave a small gift as a token of my apology to the participant and an afternoon of free consulting to the manager. The relationships were repaired, and I was left with a valuable lesson learned.

Had this manager been less astute than he was, this could have been a very costly outcome to me and the training company. My initial reaction to the participant, which came straight from my mental judgment, created a negative situation; however, my response to the negative scenario I created, came from a balance of mental reasoning and a heartfelt compassionate apology that reversed the situation and turned it back into a positive one.

Since that time, I've made a pact with myself as to the number of weeks I can effectively maintain my work without a break from long air flights, changes in time zones, and the energy extended in delivering consecutive workshops in which I strive to do the very best and model what I teach. This pact was again a balance of reasoning from the mind and compassion for myself from the heart.

My story brings several points to highlight:

- There are specific parts of behavior we all demonstrate, and each part has a positive and negative aspect to it. As a trainer, part of my job is to "control and guide" a group of individuals through a training program. That's positive. However, I crossed the line and moved to the negative aspect of controlling when I judged the participant and responded in a way that was rude and unkind. There are also parts of behavior that are more associated with the human heart. Examples of these are when we are nurturing, caring and empathetic. Whether we display those behaviors with others or to ourselves, they're heartfelt and tend to bring about more positive than negative results in our interactions.

- In each workshop there's the content of the workshop I deliver, which is the business side. It's the mental side that comes from the mind or the head. There's also the way I connect with the participants in my delivery of the workshop that can be positive or negative, which is more of the personal side. This is true of any interaction one has with a potential client, a current customer, as well as those one serves internally within the company in which one is employed. This comes from a place of compassion or the heart. It's important to maintain an awareness of what we say and how we say it.

- The words one chooses to use have a negative or positive impact. As seen in my story, one word in itself made a difference. There are specific phrases as well as full sentences and conversations that can reverse a negative situation, or keep us on a positive route to earning the highest marks from our external customers and the co-workers we serve. Some phrases to avoid with customers are "you have to," "you need to," and "you should." Who in our life told us the most what we have to, need to and should do? Right, our parents did, and most people who hear those words tell me it can make the hair stand up on the back of their necks! It's condescending to speak in this way to your customers. What we can substitute it with is "it's helpful, important, or valuable to…" or "When you do (this)…you will receive/see/find (that)." You can fill in the this and the that with whatever situation you're attending to with the customer.

- Our tone of voice and body language make up 93 percent of the impact of any interaction. Because of my lack of awareness in the moment, I don't actually remember but can now imagine that my word of "obviously" was most likely and unfortunately accompanied by a tone that exacerbated the situation. Among others, there are voice tones that sound accusing, offensive or discounting coming from the judging part of our mind. There are also the caring, nurturing, empathetic tones that come from the heart.

- The stress levels in our lives, be it work, relationships, health, the state of the world, all have an influence on our ability to remain in a state of mind and heart that best serves those we deal with in our work from day to day. Sometimes we can reason or rationalize our stress into ways of coping. An example of that would be telling ourselves in the middle of a stressful project that we only have X amount of time left and relate it to another time we successfully completed a similar project, which can help us continue working. When we look to being in balance between the head and the heart, coming from the compassionate heart will ensure we are physically and emotionally taken care of as well. We may plan from the beginning to include breaks, nurturing, healthy food, water, exercise and sufficient rest in our schedule.

- And, lastly, when we do trip and fall on our sword in the way of an error, it's important to own up to the mistake, apologize and atone in some way as I did with the gift and free coaching. Most people are forgiving and when they can see our apology is sincere and we have done something to make up for our mishap, they're more likely to not only forgive but in time to forget.

Every interaction can have an impact on the company's bottom line. Sometimes it's one person interacting directly to an external prospect or current customer. It can also be a chain of events as in a payroll clerk negatively interacting with a manager who in turn passes the negativity on to the front-line employee who passes it on to the external customer who decides not to do business with your company. It emphasizes the importance of every employee in the company practicing the positive aspects of behaviors, using productive body language, voice tones and words, and communicating from a balance of the mind and the heart.

So the responsibility for each employee to maintain a balance of being in their head and their heart can affect every interaction and subsequently the bottom line every day. Teach your employees how to maintain that balance, and you'll find the results will impact every aspect of your business in a positive way. There's an art to effective communications, and the art contains a balance of using the mind in our heads and the compassionate caring in our hearts. I end with this quote from a former CEO of IBM, Thomas J. Watson, *"To be successful have your heart in your business and your business in your heart."*

About J.L. (Jani)

J.L. (Jani) Ashmore believes in the motto, "Variety is the spice of life!" In addition to her corporate work as a speaker, coach and consultant, she has had a passion for creating and officiating wedding ceremonies. She also has a passion for studying alternative health care.

In the corporate world, Jani has trained, coached and consulted with hundreds of companies in North America, Europe and Asia Pacific. She has spoken on such topics as sales, customer service, leadership and management, empowerment and team building.

She has traveled to more than 30 countries experiencing and discovering different cultures and religions. She has tested her ability to stretch herself throughout her adult life and has, among other things, earned a black belt in karate, walked on fire, ran a marathon, hiked the Grand Canyon from rim to rim, and swam with dolphins in the wild.

Jani has had the good fortune to study closely with such teachers as Tony Robbins, Byron Katie, Jack Canfield and James Malinchak as well as others. Her commitment to her own personal and spiritual growth is innate in her and continues to broaden her life experiences. Jani's proudest accomplishment in her life, however, is seeing the beautiful, responsible, loving woman her daughter, Tamara, has grown to be and now her two blossoming granddaughters, Laurel and Calli.

She was raised in a simple environment on a dairy farm in Colorado and doesn't hold herself as an expert or guru. What she does claim to have done is to live her life to the fullest with the resources and gifts with which she was born and has developed through study and work in her varied areas of interest.

For more information about Jani and her offerings, visit her websites at www.coaching4balance.com and www.JLAshmore.com.

CHAPTER 26

Turn Obstacles Into Opportunities to Live Your Dream

By Gerald Meunier

There once was a man who had always wanted to write a novel. Having read many of the greats like Ernest Hemingway, he possessed a strong desire to write something that would contribute to a better understanding of what some called "the human condition."

Growing up and then as a young man, he thought politics was simply for politicians. One day he woke up and realized something had gone wrong. The country didn't seem the same anymore.

While this man did his part as a patriotic American—serving in the military, raising a family, working to support them, voting, eventually starting his own business in pursuit of the American dream—he assumed that politicians in Washington, DC, always looked out for the country's best interests. After all, they had sworn an oath to protect, defend and uphold the Constitution.

Just like everyone else, life kept him busy and left him with very little of his precious time to keep tabs on what politicians did. When it came time to vote for his congressional district's representative and his state's senators to go to Washington, he almost always voted for the incumbent. After all, he or she was familiar. Plus, candidates inevitably talked about fighting for local interests, and the incumbent was in the best position to do that, since that person was already in Washington. It was easier to just vote for the person already in office. It required less time to think about how to vote.

Meanwhile, as this patriotic citizen lived his life, he experienced the usual ups and downs of the economy. Each time the country went into recession, it made life very uncomfortable for him, his business and his family. By the third recession, it dawned on him that he hadn't been paying enough attention to what was happening in the country, Washington, DC, in particular. If he had, he would have been better prepared for economic cycles.

He became vaguely aware that political forces could affect businesses and that the country's problems had worsened. Although it appeared that representatives in Washington had looked out for themselves, was anyone looking out for the best interests of America?

He recollected learning American history in high school, about the Constitution, and a lot of other stuff he'd taken for granted or forgotten. His newfound awareness and concern for the country overshadowed his literary ambition. Instead of writing that novel, he explored writing a nonfiction book dealing with America's political gridlock. The fact that a nonfiction book could find a publisher before it would have to be fully written appealed to him from a business perspective. All he had to do was research everything he wanted to write about, do an outline and a proposal, and possibly one or two chapters.

It would also help to achieve the writing credentials essential to attracting a literary agent and a publisher. Realizing he hadn't published anything yet, he wrote short stories with that in mind. Getting one of his early stories published buoyed him.

By that time, he had spent several months doing research for the book he hoped would make people more aware of the problems America's politicians had caused. Then he discovered there was this thing publishers wanted called a "platform." It didn't matter how well-researched his book would be or how passionate or eloquent he could write, he needed a platform and he didn't have one. He didn't stand a chance of getting it published.

Despite that major disappointment, he turned his passions to short stories once again. Though he still wanted to write a novel, he felt he should spend some time developing his writing craft, all the while keeping his main objective clear. While doing so, he pondered the fate of the country and whether or not he could ever write anything that could make a difference.

During this period of about two years, his interest in politics intensified. The path on which the country was headed bothered him. For the first time he recognized the "dirty little secret" politicians from both major political parties didn't want citizens to know about.

They didn't care about protecting the border with Mexico. They didn't want to stop people from sneaking into America because they hoped these illegals, most of whom were Hispanic, would eventually become voters. The political party that could win them over with amnesty and free benefits would gain a huge advantage over the other party.

The political stakes were high, not to mention the threat of terrorists crossing the border. But the media hardly ever mentioned that possibility.

It disgusted him to see that politicians couldn't be trusted to do the right thing for the country. Politicians had put their own self-interests above the law and ahead of national security. There must be a way for him to speak out. But how?

It was late 2006 when everything seemed to come together. He'd been researching what type of novel to write when the idea hit him. What if he could do both—write about political issues while dramatizing their effects on regular Americans? But how could he do it and still write a commercially viable novel? The answer: "Write a political thriller!"

He knew how hard it can be to write an interesting 3,000-word short story, but a novel? He faced writing 90,000 to 110,000 words—a monumental project for a first-time novelist.

Knowing instinctively that he should network with other writers, he joined Rocky Mountain Fiction Writers. A few months later, he was accepted into two of their critique groups and began writing the first draft of his novel. He felt confident he was in good hands. As he submitted portions of his own manuscript, he experienced how torturous it can be to hear other writers tear your pride and joy to pieces. Each session left him more frustrated, but deep inside he knew that some of the criticism was warranted.

Feeling that something was lacking in the critique groups since none of the other writers had published a political thriller, he submitted part of the manuscript to a contest sponsored by Pikes Peak Writers. The comments that came back from the judges proved he had talent.

It was a turning point. That positive spark and the encouragement from a close friend was all he needed to quit his job to write full time.

Twelve months later, he wondered if he had made a mistake. He had managed to write only 30,000 more words for a total of 45,000. He wondered if he'd ever get to the 90,000-word minimum agents and publishers expected.

Meanwhile, the 2008 presidential campaign had begun. The political gridlock in Washington, DC, was exceeded only by the financial crisis. Things went from bad to worse. He was more determined than ever to be heard, but he knew he wasn't ready.

It felt as if he had hit a wall. The novel had morphed at least three times because of the multiple themes and plots associated with the border, Islamic terrorism and illegal immigration. It became impossible to focus. He stopped writing to assess the manuscript. Following his instincts, he analyzed what he had written thus far and then he developed a new outline that helped him see what needed to transpire for the novel to reach its predetermined climax.

Within a few weeks he began writing again. Words flowed freely through his fingers to the keyboard and onto the computer screen. Suddenly he was writing three times as many words per day as he used to and soon exceeded 90,000 words.

Six months later, the manuscript had been revised, edited and pitched to more than a dozen literary agents. Eight requested a partial of the manuscript, and of those, three requested the full manuscript. None offered representation.

Taking their comments and reading between the lines, he knew he was close to getting published. All he had to do was fix what the agents had found lacking.

Wanting a change, he moved from Colorado to the small town of Cody, Wyoming. It surprised him to discover a flourishing writing community.

He found three volunteers after letting people know that he was looking for readers to provide feedback on his manuscript.

They proved invaluable; however, the publishing world had changed significantly in the years since he'd started the novel. Now the first thing agents wanted to know was if he had a website and was he on Facebook and Twitter. He had none of these to offer and realized that the odds of attracting an agent and subsequently a major publishing house had turned against him.

Refusing to be deterred, he soon made a deal with a small publisher. His political thriller would be titled *Rogue Patriot.*

The book-signing party on the release date was a smashing success. Comments he later received from people who'd read the book indicated he was onto something. But he realized that without major publicity he wouldn't be able to reach enough people to make an impact. With a worsening political situation and the 2012 presidential election fast approaching, he desperately wanted to be involved in the national dialogue. He wanted to "make a difference," somehow.

Doing his best to make up for lost time in marketing and publicity, he worked at building a following on Facebook and Twitter, and started a blog. He attended conferences and networked with people he'd met.

Most people expressed support and were happy that he voiced their concerns. Before long, he realized that what he wanted to do was speak before larger groups of people about the important political issues Americans faced. It wasn't enough that he had started a second political thriller. He wanted to do more.

Finally it hit him. He had published a book, was writing a blog, and developing a social media presence. He now possessed a platform from which to build something, but what? How?

He was invited to a conference where he could meet successful people who had already built a national presence. Some of them spoke about positioning and branding. Trusting his instincts, he associated himself with people who could help him do just that.

The brand that resulted out of this journey to success is "America's Rogue Patriot." It became a natural outgrowth for Gerald Meunier, the man this chapter is about and the author of the political thriller, *Rogue Patriot.*

Gerald Meunier *is* "America's Rogue Patriot." His brand is generating buzz and speaking opportunities nationwide.

What can *you* learn from Gerald's story? He breaks it down into two areas.

First, the 10 things he practiced to achieve success are worth writing down and placing on your desk or on your wall:

1. Have a vision.
2. Develop a strategy to get there.
3. Write it down.
4. Share it with people you trust.
5. Adjust your plan when necessary.
6. Learn from the successes (and failures) of others.
7. Surround yourself with only positive-thinking people.
8. Grab hold of celebrity coattails.
9. Trust your instincts.
10. Be a player—take action.

Second, the 8 things you must do to preserve *your* American dream:

1. Be aware—what goes on in government can affect your business.
2. Get involved—you can't afford to be a bystander.
3. Don't believe everything in the media—search for the truth.
4. Read the Constitution (and the Federalist Papers)—it's actually interesting reading. You can no longer take it for granted—you owe it to yourself and to the country to be educated on the principles under which America was founded. Then you'll be amazed at what the federal government has done and is trying to do that are barriers to success. If left unchecked, our own government will jeopardize the freedoms and liberties we've all taken for granted.
5. Attend local or online discussion groups about the

Constitution. They're everywhere. Or start your own.

6. Always remember, patriotism is upholding what made America great—the Constitution.

7. Vote.

8. Make a difference—be a *Rogue Patriot.*

I look forward to meeting you at one of my speaking engagements. When you hear that "America's Rogue Patriot" is coming to a town near you, be there!

About Gerald

Author and speaker Gerald Meunier *is* "America's Rogue Patriot."

Not content with sitting on the sidelines, watching our country slip further into decline, Gerald took action. After years of research into our dysfunctional political process, he's now one of America's leading authorities on politics and government reform.

He's the author of the fast-paced political thriller, *Rogue Patriot*, and author of the forthcoming "Save America Action Plan."

Gerald enjoys speaking to people and organizations throughout the United States about today's important political issues dealing with America's debt and spending crises, border security, illegal immigration and the U.S. Constitution.

Prior to his career as a speaker and author, Gerald achieved success in marketing and business, culminating with a successful career at a publicly traded internet firm.

Originally from mountainous western Massachusetts, his love of hiking, backpacking and mountain climbing led him to Colorado where he became a leader in the Colorado Mountain Club (CMC). The CMC quarterly, *Trails & Timberline*, was the first to publish one of his stories. Other stories appear in the anthology *From the Heart*, published by Write On Wyoming in the state in which he now lives.

He's an active member of numerous organizations, including International Thriller Writers (ITW), Write On Wyoming (WOW), Rocky Mountain Fiction Writers (RMFW), and a member/leader in the CMC. He's also a member of Lions International.

To book Gerald for a speaking engagement for your group, email: pr@geraldmeunier. com. To learn more, visit Gerald at www.AmericasRoguePatriot.com.

CHAPTER 27

Creating Your Customer's Wow Experience With Humor!

By Elaine Williams

The customer's always…crazy?

I mean right…right?

Customer service is on the rocks (lemon or lime, ha-ha). Our culture continues to run faster and faster. People are multitasking and working harder than ever before, but where are we going? Even though we have more ways of communication than our grandparents ever thought possible, many people feel disconnected, dismissed or misunderstood.

I don't know about you, but I've had many bad encounters with employees at certain stores. I can't say their actual names, but places that rhyme with Gnome Repo, Hole Rudes, even the bank that rhymes with Pace (I could go on, but I won't). I've felt like I could have been on fire, with flames shooting out of my head, and the people working at these places would have just walked right past me.

What's missing? Training, specifically, humor training. I've spent more than 30 years working in every position in service and professional industries: dental offices, real estate offices, hotels, restaurants, bars, retail stores, catering, lounges and comedy clubs.

I've been a corporate trainer for Chili's, Chuy's, the Marriott, Hard Rock Café, and Del Frisco's Steakhouse NYC; and opened restaurants in Orlando, Dallas, and New York City. I've developed training manuals and systems that focused on concept, service style, menu and points of service. Until recently, I'd never been asked to train or create any kind of humor system for customer service.

My motto is "en-laughter-ment," which broken down means enlightened and laughter. The definition of "enlightened" is to lighten up. In other words, take your job seriously but not yourself so much.

The majority of companies don't train their staff how to handle difficult guests or issues. They just assume their managers will be there to handle any problems that arise throughout the shift. But nothing could be further from the truth. A well-run establishment should have staff who are empowered to handle issues if a manager isn't readily available.

For example, at one place I worked, the policy was that if a steak was overcooked or undercooked when it was brought out to the customer, the server was supposed to notify a manager immediately and get him/her to come take the steak back to the kitchen and then bring out a new steak. Great idea, in theory, yet this restaurant was huge (three floors, four wine cellars), and oftentimes the mangers were dealing with more pressing, actual emergencies like customers who were choking, had gotten too tipsy, or were fighting with other guests (I'm not kidding about the fights!)

If a server grabbed the steak because they couldn't find a manager, they often came from a place of fear: fear that they were breaking the policy and that the guest was going to be even more upset. Because of my background in comedy, I'd say to the customer: "Whoops, I guess you didn't want to be slapped by the tail! We'll be right back with a new one," or "looks like we tried to give you Mr. Smith's steak. Sorry, let me go find yours." In the customer's world, they don't care what your policy is; they just want to get their steak fixed as soon as possible, and if you can make them laugh, they release tension and take in more oxygen, which adds to relaxation. Why more businesses aren't doing humor training boggles my mind.

People love to laugh. They love to be around other people who make them laugh. Laughter diffuses stress, anger, tension. Laughter elevates mood and energy. It makes people feel good, and they don't even know why. The next time you're at a party, watch how everyone surrounds the funny person. We're naturally attracted to fun people.

We all know that dealing with the public can be enlightening and incredibly challenging at times. Teaching your staff to have fun with your customers is paramount and a fantastic way to set yourself apart from your competition. If your clients are having fun, it's more fun for the staff as well, which adds to a fun, high-energy culture where quality employees want to work.

When I was a server, I tried to make my customers laugh right off the bat: Would you care for sparkling water, still water or tequila! (everyone has at least one bad tequila story.) This was a great "test" of the customer's energy. Did they have a sense of humor? If they laughed and said "tequila?" I knew they were ready for some fun. If they seemed shaken and squirmed when I said tequila, then I knew they needed kid gloves and I should back off a bit. If they didn't even hear what I said, then I had to shift down three gears and really tune into what they needed. Perhaps they were under a major time constraint or in a heated discussion, and the last thing they needed or wanted was a server cracking jokes. This formula was a great way to gage the energy of the table and proceed accordingly.

LAUGHTER'S EFFECTS ON THE BODY

What happens when we laugh? The serotonin levels in our brains (serotonin is the feel-good chemical) rise, along with our endorphins. Our mood and our energy state become more elevated—who doesn't want more of that? "I'll have what she's having, please!"

We change physiologically when we laugh. We stretch muscles throughout our face and body, our pulse and blood pressure go up, and we breathe faster, sending more oxygen to our tissues; which gives us energy!

"The effects of laughter and exercise are very similar."One pioneer in laughter research, William Fry, claimed it took 10 minutes on a rowing machine for his heart rate to reach the level it would after just one minute of hearty laughter.

Here are more of laughter's effects on the body:
- **Blood flow:** Researchers at the University of Maryland studied the effects on blood vessels when people were shown either comedies or dramas. After the screening, the blood

vessels of the group who watched the comedy behaved normally—expanding and contracting easily. But the blood vessels in people who watched the drama tended to tense up, restricting blood flow. Did you catch that? Just say no to the drama queens!

- **Immune response:** Increased stress is associated with decreased immune system response. Studies have shown that the ability to use humor raises the level of infection-fighting antibodies in the body and boosts the levels of immune cells.

- **Blood sugar levels:** One study of 19 people with diabetes looked at the effects of laughter on blood sugar levels. After eating, the group attended a tedious lecture. The next day, the group ate the same meal and then watched a comedy. After the comedy, the group had lower blood sugar levels than they did after the lecture.

What does all this mean? Don't lecture to your staff—talk with them, joke with them, laugh together at the issues your team is dealing with. That brings me to my next point.

Acknowledgement and appreciation: We all crave it, need it, gotta have it. People won't remember what you said but how you made them feel. This is a cornerstone for any guest or client interaction with any aspect of your business.

DON'T FORGET YOUR "OTHER CUSTOMERS"

OK, maybe you're great with greeting your clients, patients or customers, but what about your inner clients: your staff? Do you greet them and pump them up for their day? Do you thank them for a good job at the end of the day?

Studies indicate that employees who feel appreciated work harder and go the extra mile for guests because they feel taken care of and respected by their superiors. What's your company's culture?

Put yourself and your staff in your customer's world. One of the most common questions I get from managers and staff is how do you keep it fresh, day after day? My answer is always, you guessed it, humor! How often do you have fun staff meetings that incorporate play and add energy to the culture?

Play with your staff and have them act out roles and really be in their customer's world. I love teaching how to really read the guest's energy state and be able to match and mirror it. A true master can anticipate their guest's needs before they even know what they want and change energy states throughout their customer experience. Are they in a hurry and need to know that you understand that and will act accordingly? Do they want to take their time and not be interrupted much? Are they bored with each other and are dying to talk to someone else.

When was the last time you encountered someone going above and beyond to make your customer service experience special? Did you share it with your team?

Bottom line is that humor, comedy and laughter can become a part of your company culture. The good news is that comedy is a muscle, and if it's worked out, it can grow. I'll share places to find simple but hilarious tools to make any meeting fun. I can also show you how to deal with having to play therapist for your employees by using humor.

When you went to business or management school, you didn't plan on becoming a therapist/counselor for your employees, did you? If you can't laugh at the paradox of that, what can you laugh at?

In conclusion, remember that the customer's always…crazy…I mean right. When your staff won't listen to you, don't take it personally; it's more about the fact that "Daddy never listened." And tequila in their coffee at the Monday meeting is great for morale!

HOSPITALITY WITH HEART

What do you get in my Hospitality With Heart Training? Here's an excerpt.

Train your staff so they can deal in case you're handling a real emergency:

1. Apologize even if it had nothing to do with you or your department. Take responsibility and genuinely show that you care about their experience.

2. Work with your team so that they are masters at warmly greeting and creating instant rapport. I wasn't the best waitress at times. I'd forget last-minute changes often. My table maintenance wasn't always spot on. However, I had

one of the highest tip ratios because of my personality, ability to read and anticipate what my guests needed and wanted, and I was able to shift and match their energy as the meal progressed. The minute I stepped into their view my energy radiated "I'm going to take care of you, so you can relax. I got this. We're going to have some fun." If they were entertaining, I'd assure them that I'd make them look good.

3. Here are two scenarios you can act out with your staff: Have two waiters sit in a booth and pretend to be having an intense business conversation while three other waiters are standing too close to the booth and having inappropriate conversations…see how distracting it is. Repeat the scenario but have your "customers" be on an important date while staff members are joking around and being unprofessional in the sight of the customer.

There's more where that came from! Sign up for my *Funny Sells!* newsletter and receive free reports like *Laughter: Releases Negativity/Burns Calories, Knock Your Socks Off Customer Service/Moments of Greatness,* and *Horrible/Funny Customer Service Stories.*

Here's the take-away: Always remind yourself you're not performing brain surgery. That's why I train your staff to take their jobs seriously but not themselves. Here's to more love and laughter in your business and life!

For more fun tips, go to www.ElaineWilliamsInspires.com.

About Elaine

With more than 30 years of experience in customer service, Elaine Williams has been a top trainer for companies such as Marriott, Hard Rock Café, Del Frisco's Steakhouse (the highest grossing restaurant in the United States), and Miller. Elaine is also a nationally touring standup comedian who has opened for Dane Cook, "Saturday Night Live's" Darrel Hammond, David Letterman favorite Dwayne Kennedy, and twice voted comic of the year, Spanky. Most recently she's been on "America's Got Talent" and the "Colbert Report." Other credits include "Saturday Night Live" with Jack Black, HBO's "Lucky Louie," Fox TV, "All My Children," "One Life to Live," and numerous commercials. She was voted Up and Coming Comic at the NY Underground Comedy Festival.

If you want to know the secret to creating raving customers who become regulars for life and tell everyone they know about your business, look no further. She's so entertaining, you won't even realize you are and your staff are learning!

Elaine's most requested topic is: "Light 'Em Up & Lead With Laughter: How to Use Humor to Motivate & Move Your Team (Even If You're Not That Funny)." She shares a professional comic's "secrets" that anyone can use to create high energy anywhere, and she teaches the "tricks" that anyone can use to "Infuse the Fun!"

To learn more about Elaine and her "Hospitality With Heart" and "Light 'Em Up With Laughter" philosophy, visit www.ElaineWilliamsInspires.com and www.ElaineWilliamsLive.com.

CHAPTER 28

A Dietitian's Insider Secrets to Guilt-Free Eating and a Healthy Weight Forever!

By Alice Baland, EatUpTheGoodLife.com

You've heard this enough yourself, I'm sure, that 67 percent of Americans—that's 2 in 3—are overweight (10 percent above Ideal Body Weight, or IBW), and about 33 percent are obese (20 percent or more above IBW). Overweight and underactive people are also more at risk for diabetes, hypertension, stroke, heart attack, sleep apnea and other health risks. Stress eating is up!

What does that mean to you? Some of my clients tell me they have no energy to play with the kids or grandkids, can't fit into stadium or airplane seats, can't fit into favorite clothes, can't catch a breath or take a flight of steps, can't sleep without a C-PAP machine, and are at risk of losing the independence and freedom that comes with health. In other words, they live in a world of "can'ts." All these problems come with enormous business, financial and family costs.

 Not that it's right, but slimmer people are more likely to get better jobs and keep them than their overweight colleagues. Slim people usually have more energy, too! They can take adventures around the world and at home without worrying if they can climb mountains or the stairs at the castles.

Therefore, millions of people are on diets to lose needed pounds to avoid deadly consequences. Bariatric surgeries are up. Diets tend to be restrictive and don't last, plus the weight tends to rebound and then some. Surgery has risks, too. What if you don't want those options? Surely there's an easier way to reach a healthy weight forever—without guilty eating. There is! Let me show you some *Dietitian Insider Secrets* that are simple, lasting, and have proven results for *Pleasurable, Guilt-Free Eating & Living!*

Would you agree with me that if you don't have your health no amount of money or prestige will make up for it? I'm passionate about health! Without health, family, life, money, your dreams cannot be wildly enjoyed!

That's how I've gone *From Cowgirl to Crusader*. As a 4-year-old in our hard-dirt apartment yard behind my dad's laundry, John Wayne was my hero as I chased the bad guys on my broomstick pony every afternoon. Now my crusade is against the bad guys who hurt our health, self-esteem, body image, intelligence and relationships!

When I was 8 years old, I observed that most classmates had a donut or no breakfast in the morning. They were tired, easily distracted and didn't learn as well. When I was 15, I was mentored by a special foods and nutrition teacher and decided to become a Registered Dietitian. Later, I became a therapist to help others in even broader ways. I've dedicated my life to learning how to heal and help others be healthy, happy and self-reliant in mind, body and spirit.

People come to me for *problems that I solve,* such as binge eating, achieving a healthy weight, personalized nutrition plans, overcoming anxiety, life balance, stopping eating disorders in children, and having a happier marriage. Without our emotional, physical and mental health, life can be really rough. I'm an achievement and completion specialist to help you win!

First, let's get a more clear understanding of what can lead to being overweight. Bet the first thing you thought of was too many calories and not enough exercise. Right, but there's more. Millions of people overeat due to stress, emotions, out of control feelings, distractions, self-doubt, a history of trauma (such as incest, sexual assault, accidents or sports injuries leading to abuse of pain medications), inadequate meal planning, not knowing what's best to eat, and improper food selection.

Too many Americans are negatively impacted by the economy, lost jobs or fewer hours, lost homes and long hours at work and travel. Many of them stress eat; others turn to alcohol, gambling, internet, drugs or shopping. What's a person to do? Do you want to do it the way you've always done it or *the right way?* Is there hope for you? Yes!

Think about *why* you want to make positive changes in your life, and I'll share some simple ways to do it. Ready?

Let me introduce you to three people who successfully reclaimed their lives and freedom from unhealthy habits. These are a composite of real clients with a few details changed to protect their confidentiality. Do you see yourself or a loved one here? Afterward, I'll give specific ideas on what you can do to avoid or improve these conditions.

SUCCESS STORY #1: JOHN

John is a happily married, successful business owner in his 50s with hypertension and pre-diabetes. He was a three-pack-per-day smoker but quit many years ago when his son was born. As a child his mother gave him what he liked, and he was always a big eater and cleaned his plate. He was active in sports at 185 pounds, but struggled after college. Over-eating is worse at night; he likes sauces, spaghetti, bread, salt, candy, ice cream and sweets. At 350 pounds and 5 feet 10, his goal was to lose 130 pounds or have bariatric surgery, but he gave himself one last chance to avoid it. When he came to me, he said, *"I liked your talk and know I need you on my team!"* I personalized his health program, and here are 6 weight-loss strategies that led to his success!

1. Since John traveled a lot on business, a major concern was what to eat at restaurants and hotels. What a positive attitude can do for anyone! At Maggiano's I recommended tilapia with spinach and tomatoes with a light lemon butter sauce and a salad with vinegar and a few drops of oil. He learned to do this at every restaurant. *"Alice, I never feel deprived, and I get full."*

2. I designed six low-salt, high-flavor meals and snacks, such as fish, salads and colorful veggies so he's not hungry. I provided him with recipes and grocery lists. He loves my meal-replacement shake of 20 grams whey protein, 8-ounce almond milk, and a half cup frozen blueberries.

3. Cognitive: John asked, *"Will I get bored? No. Can I keep up this*

pace? Is this sustainable? Yes, I like it!" I asked him to keep a self-discovery journal that would always be his personal plan to success. Like in his business, his plan was to *Decide. Focus. Achieve!* He set his goal in 25-pound increments and celebrated each week with a non-food reward.

4. Portion control is important. One cup of pasta is two bread servings versus a huge restaurant platter. Educate yourself about correct portions. Adding fiber to meals fills you up.

5. We filled up his evenings with PM Yoga, walks with his wife, card games, reading, brushing teeth, and a hobby so night eating disappeared! He decided on no food after 8 p.m. *The kitchen is closed.*

6. At work his refrigerator is filled with healthy, nutrient-dense, low-calorie foods. His self-confidence grew.

He has dropped over 90 pounds so far and feels great, plus no surgery needed! His wife, family and doctors are thrilled!

SUCCESS STORY #2: KC

KC is a 30-year-old attorney who started her first diet at age 12, has been binge eating for more than 15 years, and doesn't feel she's good enough, even though she's highly accomplished. She feels overwhelmed and incompetent at work, even though her bosses think she's great. She's not sure if she's pretty enough for her boyfriend, even when he sends roses. Even though her weight is fine for her height, her feelings of inadequacy and isolation, plus not feeling in control of her life, leads her to binge eat and drink more than 10,000 calories a day. This led to bloating, sweating, and beating herself up for yet one more thing. It doesn't help that the office often has plenty of free high-calorie comfort foods available during the day to tempt her. Her weight shot up. Fortunately, she doesn't purge and she loves to ski, run and do yoga when she can but not obsessively.

 Diets work for a while, but they can mess up your health, metabolism, and create a sense of failure and worthlessness. Guilt and regret creep in. What works instead so you can enjoy real food and reach a healthy weight forever? While eating disorders require specialized care, start with these tips.

4 Ways to Calm Chaotic/Stress/Emotional Eating

1. Breakfast is a critical meal for anyone. Have one within one to two hours of rising and make it a rich source of protein (eggs, salmon, whey protein shake), which helps prevent food cravings later in the day. Enjoy a whole grain with it, such as warm quinoa with sweet bell peppers. Including fat (a couple slices of avocado, a few almonds or a spoonful of almond butter) prevents you from craving food too fast. The right combination of protein, complex carbohydrates and healthy fat is an A+ strategy.

2. I taught KC Emotional Freedom Technique (EFT), which is like acupuncture, but without the needles. Tapping your body's energy points/meridians is Energy Psychology, which calms your subconscious mind and your body so you can quickly overcome the urge to overeat or choose the wrong foods. It works on many problems! Tap every morning, bedtime and when temptation is greatest. Do it 10 to 20 times a day! (I can show you how via Skype).

3. Create a Happy Kit to turn to during the day when stress becomes too much (see *Eat Up the Good Life!*). Include letters from those who build you up, fun pictures, favorite songs on your iPhone, a healthy snack (like buffalo jerky or fruit leather strips).

4. Increase your social support system so you can call a safe friend any time you feel the need. The more you have, the better. I find that having a variety of coaches helps me have better success in any area.

Of course, as I worked with KC over time, I taught her many more life skills she could transfer to every area of her life. I distinguish between the Two Hungers: physical hunger (satisfied by the right foods, right amounts, right times) and emotional hunger (satisfied with a healthy mindset, self-care, and my "Luscious Buffet of Self-Care Delicacies" in my book). It's also important to learn how to manage your Inner Life (thoughts, appetite) and Outer Life (work, family, friends, advertising). We also worked on self-image, relationship skills, boundaries and confidence.

KC said, *"You showed me how to recognize that every time I eat when I'm not hungry, I'm using food, not for nutrition, but as something else: a soother, a pain-killer, a remedy for fear, anxiety or boredom. Now I know what to do instead of overeat and I am satisfied."* Awesome progress!

SUCCESS STORY #3: SAMANTHA

Samantha is a 47-year-old, successful career woman just 15 to 25 pounds above her best weight. She copes with feelings, daily stresses and avoids conflict in work or her relationship with her spouse by binge eating. This keeps her from achieving her best weight and personal confidence. Shame and guilt set in, and her personal self-talk says, *"This addiction is pulling me the wrong direction. I should be able to stop. I gained weight from eating at that French restaurant. It's just one day. So what? Who am I? Why do I try to do it all then still not feel good enough? It's hard to ask others for what I really need. When I do, my husband sees this as criticism, but it's not. I harbor stress in my shoulders and stomach. I'm overwhelmed! How do I put myself first?"*

6 Top Tips for Emotional Eating

1. An unmet need, often unconscious, can lead to emotional eating, blame and shame. Ask for what you really need—in a kind, loving, yet direct, authentic way. Feel uncomfortable for a while until you get used to getting your needs met, feeling heard, and then really enjoy how confident and happy you feel!

2. Put yourself first in the respect that when you take care of your own simple needs, then you can better handle what the day throws at you. Ask for a take-home container at the beginning of meals so you can enjoy them later or share with someone else. Work out or walk 30 minutes more the day before and after you eat out. Drink 64 ounces of water a day.

3. Instead of all the cream sauces, fried items and rich desserts, ask for steamed, baked, broiled, a little bit of olive oil or butter on the side. Then relish each bite with pure pleasure! I have "65 Savvy Skills" in my *Eat Up the Good Life!* book that will really help you find your way.

4. Keep a daily *Food/Mood/Thoughts Journal* every day for 30 days to track your ups and downs. You'll get immediate feedback, and it will be helpful for your coach. Rather than demean yourself, circle a few things you'd like to change, then do one at a time. Keeping a food record can double your weight loss and awareness. You can do it!

5. Nearly everyone accumulates stress in their body. Do a self-assessment a few times a day, then take a deep breath through your nose into your

lungs; slowly exhale all the way through to your feet. Do this one minute three times a day. Notice how fast you feel more relaxed.

6. It only takes *one* person to change a family or work system. By taking 100 percent accountability for your thoughts and actions, even though it's tough at times, you'll gain inner strength and courage.

Samantha told me, *"I lost the weight I wanted after coaching with you. I'm better at confrontation and setting boundaries with the in-laws and at work. The follow-up emails after our phone sessions helped remind me of the promises I made to myself. Your easy-going, non-judgmental style allowed me to open up and have a trusting relationship with you and discuss confidential issues and challenges. I really needed regular check-ins to focus on the behavioral changes I'm trying to embed in my life. You really understand healthy eating habits, nutrition and emotional struggles in addition to your psychotherapy experience. This all came out at the right time during our sessions!"*

Earlier, I said I'd share some simple ways to make positive changes in your life. I gave you "6 Weight Loss Strategies," "4 Ways to Calm Chaotic/Stress/Emotional Eating," and "6 Top Tips for Emotional Eating." Do you agree that I kept my promise? Pick just one of these and integrate it into your life. Then pick another and another.

You, too, can achieve guilt-free eating and a healthy weight forever with your best moment-by-moment choices, taking one small step at a time. You deserve great health, because you have a special mission on Earth that only you can do in your own best way! If you want to get a fresh viewpoint and achieve even more, see my contact information below.

About Alice

Alice Baland will show you how to make smart decisions and personalized choices that will expand your life. She offers simple solutions and strategies so you can achieve greater success and happiness! She inspires hope, confidence, and positive change in audiences, clients and readers. Get her free report, audio download and crave-free meal video at www.EatUpTheGoodLife.com or www.AliceBaland.com.

Alice is the one who people seek out to permanently overcome weight concerns, eating disorders, anxiety, adversity, life's stressors, poor nutrition, body loathing and toxic relationships. She'll show you how to create a balanced, productive, energized and fun life where food isn't a struggle so you can *Eat Up The Good Life!™*

She's an expert with a proven track record—as a victor, psychotherapist and dietitian in the real world. She'll help you answer, *"Are you worth the choice? What do you do next? Would you like to crave something more than food—like self-worth, self-love and self-acceptance? Or lifelong health and a happy self-image?"* Alice will show you how to do it. She invites you to Take a Bite of the Good Life! Be your best self on the inside and beat the binge on the outside. Regain control of your eating, weight and your life.

Contact Alice's office to see if you qualify for her private coaching program or discuss how to schedule her program for your event! Laugh, Learn and Build Your Best Self! Learn about her 3D Approach to Success: *I Desire It! I Deserve It! I'm Determined to Get It!*

Alice is a medical and clinical hypnotherapist, EFT master trainer, psychotherapist, eating disorders and sports dietitian. Her books include *Eat Up the Good Life!™ Savvy Skills for Pleasurable, Guilt-Free Eating & Living; Catch Your Dreams: Getting What You Want…Now! Positive Nutrition: The Girl's GUIDE to Eating for Energy, Esteem & Excitement,* and *Positive Nutrition: Top Tips for Healthy Students.* She also offers complete home study/play programs to advance your life vision.

She has been interviewed by CNN, CBS, ABC and NBC; the *Wall Street Journal; USA Today;* and the "Dallas Morning News," to name a few. She's a former spokesperson for the American Dietetic Association and international food companies, reaching millions of Americans with her positive nutrition, health and life balance messages coast-to-coast. Add to her portfolio backpacker, distance cyclist, scuba diver, world traveler, dancer, culinary specialist and trauma survivor, and you've got the recipe for a woman with a dynamic healing program to help you be your best self!

CHAPTER 29

Creating Goals to Achieve Your Greatest Health and Wellness

By Annielette Manuel

"Happiness is a function of accepting what is. Love is a function of communication. Health is a function of participation. Self Expression is a function of responsibility."—Werner Erhard

Setting goals will help you to attain better health and meet your body's needs. *Only you are the one who knows what your values are, and only you know your body best.* Having wellness goals offers you the ability to keep focused. You'll not only save energy by eliminating wasted effort but also open your mind to finding ways to accomplish your target goal easier. Like a perfectly placed jump shot, you'll get "nothing but net" when following these *five simple steps*.

INDIVIDUALIZATION IS THE KEY

Just as no two snowflakes are alike, no two humans are the same. Even identical twins have various nuances about them that separate each other. The beauty about our uniqueness is that the same circumstance for two different people will almost always yield different results. *Different rationalization. Different action. Different outcome.* However, each may believe their decision was the right one. This is what makes humans so amazing; we possess the ability to distinguish ourselves as individuals.

WHAT ARE YOUR GOALS, AND WHAT CAN
YOU DO TO ACHIEVE THEM?

Have you ever woken up and told yourself you should be doing something to help yourself and others? One morning I woke up and wondered why I had never run a marathon. My friend Larry was training to complete the 26.2 mile run in Philadelphia to raise money for programs that help create livelihoods for villages in third-world countries. I immediately thought I should do it, too!

The problem was, I hadn't been running since high school, and I had such a sedentary lifestyle because of my 9-to-5 office job. But the thought kept at me.

Finally, I gave in and decided to do it. It was only about two months before the marathon. During this time, I looked up to Larry as he'd been training for roughly six months. He knew how to prepare. I asked him questions and told him about my plans. He thought it would be difficult for me since I hadn't been training. Nevertheless, he remained supportive. I began a training crash course, keeping myself disciplined but working out at the gym and taking the stairs instead of the elevator. At that time, my apartment was on the 12th floor! Throughout the preparation, I kept my vision in my mind. *I wanted to finish the marathon—that was my goal.*

A few days before the Philadelphia marathon, I ran part of the course. I timed myself, keeping a steady pace. I thought, this is how it's going to feel. Already I had noticed changes in my health since starting my exercise regimen. I had more stamina. I was craving healthier food. And best of all, I was feeling healthier and happier. Even if I didn't finish the whole 26 miles, I knew I would be happy with how quickly I changed for the better.

The day finally came. It was a chilly November morning. To further motivate myself to quickly finish the run, I wore a dorky running outfit consisting of spandex underarmor, running shorts, a blue baseball cap and a thin light-blue running jacket. Everyone else wore running outfits, some with just shorts and t-shirts, others with jackets and pants, and those in between. I immediately recognized the runners who had trained for months and rationalized they would likely finish first. They had on minimal clothing, just a tank top, shorts and running shoes, even though the wind chill was easily below 20 degrees. There were hundreds of people. I looked over the tents set up by the Philadelphia museum and saw *the finish line*.

This course would take me throughout the city of Philadelphia and back to the museum. I ran the course in my head and saw myself sprinting across the finish line. The marathon had begun with a single shot being fired. Each participant received a tracking device that monitored how quickly they were running and at what exact time they crossed the start and finish line. I was running with Larry for a good 10 miles or so, keeping up with his pace at roughly 9 to 10 miles per hour. I must have drank too much of the sports drinks and water the volunteers were giving out during designated stops, because I found myself stopping for a break and losing track of Larry. I ran the next 10 miles by myself, making sure to keep my pace steady. *Without Larry by my side, I noticed I was running 10 to 11 miles per hour.* Not bad, I thought; for sure I'll finish the race at a decent time.

Suddenly, I experienced a shooting pain in my foot. My run had crawled to a limping jog. I saw people around me being carted off on emergency vehicles. I remembered my goal: I will finish the run. But I was tired and in pain. I had a decision to make. I asked myself, *will I let my excuses be in control, or will I finish the marathon I prepared so hard for?* The choice was clear. I kept jogging. And as I my hamstring cramped, I modified my run to an alternating jog and power-walk combination. I also met new friends along the way, who also pushed on with cramps or injuries. *We motivated each other and kept each other going.* This continued for the last 6 miles.

Finally, we saw the bleachers lining the 100 meter dash to the finish line. I saw myself sprinting across it so that was exactly what I did! Larry and his family, as well as a couple of friends, were waiting for me at the finish line. I was so happy and grateful to have the opportunity to finish a whole marathon. I was exhausted, but I did it! *And I attribute a great part of my success to the goals I had set about two months prior.*

5 STEPS TO ACHIEVING YOUR ULTIMATE HEALTH AND WELLNESS

1. Take responsibility for your current state of being. The greatest and most empowering feeling is taking the first step. Don't be afraid to *take full responsibility for where you are and how you got there.* Know that everything you're experiencing in your body and your health is a result of actions you've taken in the past. By accepting your current state and taking responsibility for where you are now, especially in regards to your health, you're giving yourself the power to change. If you created it, then you can create something new. Know that you're in control of your body and your health!

It's equally important not to blame yourself. The *key is to be objective and nonjudgmental* throughout this introspection. What's in the past is there to stay, and you can only move forward. At this point it's important to be true to yourself. You may even ask a trusted friend, a coach or a mentor what they think you may need to change regarding your health or lifestyle. Having someone's different point of view can be crucial to seeing what needs to be done.

The following statements should give you some insights on where to start with the next process:

I feel _____ about my body.

I think my health is _____.

When I see myself in the mirror I think _____
_____.

2. Create goals. What's the perfect vision of your health? How do you view wellness as it pertains to you as an individual? How does it affect those around you? The second step is equally as important, as it sets the stage for where you'll be heading. Is your goal to have a healthier body? Or maybe to just start an exercise routine? Get a picture of what you want. Really dig deep. What would be a healthier you...for you? Everyone is different, so your own personal goal should be something that resonates with you. *Go ahead and get a clean sheet of paper and just write down whatever comes to mind regarding your health.* See if there are words or phrases that repeat themselves and form your goals around that idea.

As you refine your perfect health and wellness goals, continue to imagine it in your mind. How would you feel? How would you act? How would others around you act and treat you? Experience the end goal as happening now, if only in your mind for the time being. During this time there may be objections, such as "I can't... It's impossible... I don't have the self discipline..." Connect with these thoughts that can ultimately slow or even stop your progress. Now's the time to address them. Are you really committed to your health goal? Or will you let a few thoughts hinder you?

Here are some sample goals:

- In six months I'm my perfect weight for my body type.
- I'm eating healthy food at the caloric intake that's right for my body.
- I'm happy with my healthy body.
- My body feels great, and I have more energy daily.

The important thing with your goal is to keep what you want to accomplish in mind—not what you want to get rid of. So the goal statement "I have a slimmer body" is better than "I am losing weight" or "I am trimming fat off my waist line."

My Health and Wellness Goal(s):

_____

_____

_____

_____

3. Notice your action steps, and take inspired or motivated action!
As you begin to look at your goals in a new light, you'll automatically be drawn to action. You'll begin to notice information you might have missed before or even find that everyday ordeals have a whole new meaning. You may be inspired to take a class on qigong, or do some research regarding something specific about your health. Another action step that you find yourself doing is following a guru or mentor, someone who has already done what you seek to do yourself.

These are inspired actions, which are different from motivated actions. Inspired action often creates lasting results more often than motivated action. When you're inspired, you're acting from your heart, your intuition. Motivated action stems from the mind and the rational centers of the body. Often New Year's resolutions are from motivated action and thus in a few months the goal is lost. If you have a partner you are working with on the goal, then it's easier to sustain motivated action.

What are my inspired actions? (List things that come to mind during the day—or better yet just do them!)

_____

_____

_____

_____

What motivated actions should I take? (These can be action steps or initial planning that you can do.)

_____

_____

_____

_____

If you have trouble taking inspired action, or even noticing what inspires you, it's important that a coach or mentor is there to support you. There are going to be distractions and times when inspiration or motivation might be low, when thoughts might steer you away from your goal. Even just having a partner that's supportive and will remind you about your goals in a nonjudgmental way can help greatly when the going gets tough.

Who are my support people? Who can I turn to for help or motivation?

_____   _____

_____   _____

_____   _____

4. Review results. Have you noticed any changes in your life? Are you feeling happier and healthier? Keep a notebook or a blog of all the differences you or others notice in your life. It can be as small as a change in posture, or noticing that you're taking deeper breaths. Or you may notice that you feel less stress during the day. Review the results you're getting. If need be, modify your goals or your action steps. There may be times when your goals open up a new area of your life that you would like to change. For example, as a result of eating healthier for a few weeks, you've been having more energy and thus would like to create an exercise routine, whereas in the past you may not have had enough energy at the end or beginning of the day.

Keep a journal or even a word document of what transpires each day. You'll be able to gain insights, as well as use the small daily accomplishments as fuel for your growth. If you're open to sharing your journal with a trusted friend, then it's even better, as your friend can sometimes share insights you yourself may have missed.

5. Enjoy and have fun! The final—and probably the best step—is to enjoy your new healthy body and have fun! This is your life and your body, and you deserve it. Take the time to do things you've always wanted to do, like a sport or hobby. Love your body and love how terrific your health is!

You can use these steps for any aspect of your life. Maintaining a healthy balance in your life includes reducing daily stress, eating a healthy diet and starting an exercise regimen that's right for you. Each body is different, so each need must be addressed individually. The best thing to do is to feel great now, then notice what it is you do that makes you feel even better.

To your greatest health!
If you ever feel there's something in your body that doesn't feel right, please contact your primary physician or health care provider. There are also wellness visits that you can set up, which are now supported by most insurance. These visits can help you to learn more about your current level of health, as well as which exercises to do and what kind of diet to follow. You can find out about wellness visits from your insurance provider or primary care physician.

About Annielette

Annielette's passion is to heal, improve and transform the lives of others, and her own in the process. She's currently a certified NLP practitioner, certified life coach, and registered nurse in the state of New Jersey. She has used and researched various health modalities as well as personal development courses for over seven years and has improved her life as well as the lives of those around her.

She has completed her BSN from Drexel University and her NLP Master Practitioner as well as life coach certification from the American University of NLP.

Annielette is part of the American Holistic Nurses Association, the Global Sciences Foundation, and the National Center for Homeopathy.

If you liked the information presented here or would like to learn more about how life coaching can improve your health and wellness, simply visit annielette.com or email info@annielette.com. You can also add "annielette" on Skype. Annielette is offering a free 30-minute consulting session; simply mention *Nothing But Net* in your correspondence.